CW00894710

The Ultimate Air Fryer Cookbook UK

The Budget Friendly and Yummy Air Fryer Meals for Beginners With Easy to Follow Instructions to Air Fry, Bake (2023 Edition)

Ludie M. Linger

Copyright© 2022 By Ludie M. Linger All Rights Reserved

This book is copyright protected. It is only for personal use. You cannot amend, distribute, sell, use, quote or paraphrase any part of the content within this book, without the consent of the author or publisher.

Under no circumstances will any blame or legal responsibility be held against the publisher, or author, for any damages, reparation, or monetary loss due to the information contained within this book, either directly or indirectly.

Disclaimer Notice:

Please note the information contained within this document is for educational and entertainment purposes only. All effort has been executed to present accurate, up to date, reliable, complete information. No warranties of any kind are declared or implied. Readers acknowledge that the author is not engaged in the rendering of legal, financial, medical or professional advice. The content within this book has been derived from various sources. Please consult a licensed professional before attempting any techniques outlined in this book.

By reading this document, the reader agrees that under no circumstances is the author responsible for any losses, direct or indirect, that are incurred as a result of the use of the information contained within this document, including, but not limited to, errors, omissions, or inaccuracies.

Contents

Chapter 8 Vegetables and Sides 62

The Airfryer Discovery

I was really skeptical about air fryers at first. I thought they were just a fad and that they couldn't possibly live up to the hype. But then a friend of mine got one and they raved about it, so I decided to give it a try. I'm so glad I did!

The air fryer is amazing. I've already used it to make all sorts of delicious meals. Chicken, fish, vegetables, French fries… you name it, the air fryer can cook it. And everything comes out crispy and golden brown, without any oil. It's incredible!

If you're thinking about getting an air fryer, or if you've already got one and are looking for some new recipes to try, definitely check out this cookbook. It's packed with easy-to-follow recipes for all sorts of delicious air fried foods.

How does it work?

An air fryer is a small appliance that uses convection to circulate hot air around food, resulting in a crispy, fried texture without all the oil of traditional frying methods. This cookbook contains recipes that are designed specifically for air fryers, so you can get the most out of your new appliance.

Air frying is a healthier alternative to deep frying because it uses less oil and results in less fat absorption by the food. Additionally, air fryers cook food more evenly than other methods, so you can expect consistent results with each batch.

In this air fryer cookbook for beginners, we'll show you how to make some of your favourite recipes in an air fryer. From starters to main courses to desserts, we've got you covered.

We'll also give you some tips on how to use your air fryer to its full potential. Trust us, once you start cooking with an air fryer, you'll never go back!

Not only are our recipes easy to follow, but they're also affordable and quick to make. So, if you're looking for a healthy way to cook your food, then be sure to continue reading our air fryer cookbook!

6 main features of the Airfryer

Airfryers are designed with a range of features to make cooking easier and more enjoyable. Here are six of the main features to look for when choosing an airfryer:

1. Temperature control

Most airfryers will have a temperature control feature, which allows you to set the perfect cooking temperature for your food. This is especially useful for ensuring that your food is cooked evenly.

2. Timer

Many airfryers come with a timer, so you can set it to start cooking at a specific time. This is great for ensuring that your food is cooked perfectly, without any risk of overcooking or undercooking.

3. Capacity

Most airfryers have a capacity of 2-4 litres, meaning they can cook a good amount of food at once. This is perfect for feeding a family or group of friends.

4. Automatic shut off

Some airfryers come with an automatic shut off feature, which helps to prevent overcooking and ensures your safety while using the appliance.

5. Non-stick coating

Many airfryers have a non-stick coating, which makes cleanup quick and easy. This also helps to prevent sticking and burning, making your cooking experience more enjoyable.

6. Dishwasher safe

Another convenient feature found in some airfryers is that they are dishwasher safe, meaning all you need to do is put them in the dishwasher!

Foods to cook the Airfryer

The airfryer is a versatile kitchen appliance that can be used to cook a variety of different foods. Here are some of the best foods to cook in the airfryer and why they can be cooked in it:

1. Chicken wings

Chicken wings can be cooked in the airfryer without any oil, making them a healthier option than traditional fried chicken wings. The airfryer will also help to keep the chicken wings crispy on the outside while still being juicy on the inside.

2. French fries

French fries can also be cooked in the airfryer without any oil. This makes them a healthier alternative to traditional deep-fried french fries. The airfryer will help to keep the french fries crispy on the outside while still being soft on the inside.

3. Vegetables -

Vegetables can be cooked in the airfryer with or without oil. If you are looking for a healthier option, you can cook your vegetables without any oil. The airfryer will help to keep your vegetables crisp and fresh tasting.

4. Fish -

Fish can be cooked in the airfryer with or without oil. If you are looking for a healthier option, you can cook your fish without any oil. The air fryer will help to keep your fish moist and tender while still getting that nice crispy exterior.

5. Desserts

Air frying is a great way to cook desserts! You can use your air fryer to make all sorts of delicious desserts, from cakes and cookies to brownies and pies.

Here are some tips for making desserts in your air fryer:

1. Preheat your air fryer before you start cooking. This will help ensure that your dessert cooks evenly.

2. Use a light coating of oil or cooking spray on your desserts to prevent them from sticking to the air fryer basket.

3. Cook your desserts at a lower temperature than you would normally cook them at in an oven. This will prevent them from burning or drying out

4. Check on your desserts regularly while they are cooking, and remove them from the air fryer when they are done. With these tips, you can make all sorts of delicious desserts in your air fryer!

Foods to avoid in the Airfryer

There are some foods that just don't belong in the airfryer.

Here's a list of foods not to cook in the airfryer, and why:

1. Wet or soggy foods

Foods that are wet or soggy will not cook

evenly in the airfryer and may end up sticking to the basket.

2. Breaded foods

The breading on foods like chicken nuggets or fish sticks can become too crispy in the airfryer, making them unpleasant to eat.

3. Delicate fruits and vegetables

Fruits and vegetables like grapes, tomatoes, and mushrooms can be easily overcooked or even burnt in the airfryer. Stick to harder fruits and vegetables like apples and carrots.

4. Foods with sauces or gravies

Sauces and gravies can splatter and make a mess in the airfryer, so it's best to avoid them altogether.

5. Greasy foods –

Finally, you want to be careful with foods that have a lot of fat or oil. These can cause your air fryer to smoke and potentially start a fire. So, while you may be tempted to cook up some bacon, it's best to avoid it in your air fryer.

8 Benefits of Cooking with an Airfryer

1. Air fryers cook food quickly and evenly.

Air fryers cook food quickly and evenly. This is due to the fact that air fryers circulate hot air around the food, cooking it evenly on all sides. Additionally, air fryers can reach high temperatures very quickly, meaning that your food will cook faster than it would in a traditional oven.

2. Air fryers use little to no oil, making them a healthier option than traditional frying methods.

Air fryers work by circulating hot air around food that has been coated in a small amount of oil. This produces a crispy, fried-like texture without all the excess oil and fat found in traditional frying methods. Not only is this healthier for you, but it also means that food cooked in an air fryer is often less greasy and easier to digest.

Air fryers are a great option for those looking to cut down on their oil intake or cook healthier meals. They can be used to cook a variety of foods, from chicken and fish to vegetables and even desserts. And because they use less oil, air fryers typically produce less smoke and odor than deep fryers, making them a safer option for cooking at home.

3. Air fryers are easy to use and clean.

When it comes to using an air fryer, the process is pretty simple. All you have to do is add your food to the fryer basket, set the temperature, and let it cook.

The great thing about air fryers is that they come with preset cooking times and temperatures, so all you have to do is press a button and walk away. When your food is done, the air fryer will shut off automatically.

When it comes to cleaning an air fryer, the process is just as simple. Most air fryers have a non-stick coating on their baskets and pans, so all you need to do is wipe them down with a damp cloth after each use. If there are any stubborn bits of food stuck on, you can use a soft bristled brush to remove them. And that's it! An air fryer is one of the easiest kitchen appliances to use and clean.

4. Air fryers can be used to cook a variety of foods, including chicken, fish, vegetables, and French fries.

Air fryers are a versatile kitchen appliance that can be used to cook a variety of foods. Chicken, fish, and vegetables can all be cooked in an air fryer, and French fries are a popular choice as well. Air fryers work by circulating hot air around the food, which cooks it evenly and prevents it from sticking to the bottom of the pan. This makes air fryers a healthier option than deep-frying, as there is no need for oil.

5. Air fryers can help you save money on your grocery bill.

Air fryers can help you save money on your grocery bill by allowing you to cook at home more often. Instead of eating out or ordering in, you can cook your own meals with an air fryer. This can help you save money on both food and beverage costs. Additionally, air fryers can help you reduce your food waste because you can cook smaller portions as needed. This can help you save money on groceries by reducing the amount of food that you need to purchase.

6. Air fryers are small and compact, making them perfect for small kitchens or apartments.

Air fryers are small and compact, making them perfect for small kitchens or apartments. They don't require any extra space like a traditional oven or stovetop, so you can save valuable counter space. Additionally, air fryers use less energy than other cooking methods, so they're perfect for those who want to save on their energy bill.

7. Air fryers are available in a variety of sizes and designs to suit your needs.

Air fryers come in all shapes and sizes, from small countertop models to larger freestanding units. No matter what your needs are, there's an air fryer out there that's perfect for you.

Small air fryers are great for couples or small families who want to enjoy the benefits of air frying without taking up a lot of counter space. If you entertain often or have a large family, a larger air fryer is the way to go.

Some air fryers even come with multiple cooking baskets, so you can cook multiple items at once. When it comes to design, there are plenty of options to choose from as well. If you want an air fryer that looks sleek and modern, there are plenty of options available. Or, if you prefer something with a more traditional look, you can find those as well. No matter what your style is, you're sure to find an air fryer that fits right in with your kitchen décor.

8. Air fryers come with a variety of features, such as timers and adjustable temperature controls, to make cooking easier and more convenient

Air fryers come with a variety of features, such as timers and adjustable temperature controls, to make cooking easier and more convenient. For those who are short on time, an air fryer can be a real lifesaver.

You can set the timer for the desired cooking time and walk away, knowing that your food will be cooked perfectly every time. Another great feature of air fryers is the adjustable temperature control.

This allows you to cook your food at the perfect temperature, ensuring that it is cooked through without being burnt. No more worrying about whether your food is overcooked or undercooked – with an air fryer, you can be confident that it will be just right.

Cleaning your Airfryer

Assuming you have an air fryer that is in need of cleaning, here are the steps you should take to clean it:

1. First and foremost, unplug your air fryer from the outlet. You don't want to be working with any electrical appliances while they are still plugged in.

2. Next, you will want to remove the basket from the air fryer. Most models will have a removable basket that can easily be taken out.

3. Once the basket is removed, empty any remaining food or debris that may be inside of it.

4. After the basket is emptied, you can begin washing it with warm soapy water. Be sure to scrub any areas that look like they may need a little extra attention.

5. Once the basket is clean, set it aside and begin cleaning the interior of the air fryer itself. Again, use warm soapy water to wipe down the inside of the appliance. If there are any stubborn spots, you can use a soft sponge or brush to help remove them.

6. After you have cleaned the interior of the air fryer, dry it off with a clean towel before moving on to

7. The final step is to replace the filter (if your model has one). This filter helps to keep food particles from entering into the fan area and causing damage over time. To replace it, simply remove the old filter and insert a new one.

Maintaining your Airfryer

If you're like most people, you probably don't think much about maintaining your air fryer. But, just like any other kitchen appliance, your air fryer needs a little TLC from time to time to keep it running smoothly.

Here are a few tips to help you maintain your air fryer and keep it in tip-top shape:

Clean the basket regularly - The basket is where the food goes in the air fryer, so it's important to keep it clean. Wipe it down with a damp cloth after each use and give it a more thorough cleaning every few weeks.

Don't overfill the basket - It's important not to overfill the basket when using your air fryer. This can cause uneven cooking and even fires. So, make sure to read the instructions carefully and only put as much food in the basket as

recommended.

Keep an eye on the oil - If you're using oil in your air fryer, be sure to check it regularly and replenish as needed. Too much or too little oil can both cause problems, so it's important to keep an eye on it.

Clean the outside of the unit - The outside of the unit can get dirty over time from splatters and grease build-up. Wipe it down with a damp cloth regularly to keep it clean and looking its best.

Check for cracks or damage - Inspect your air fryer

10 Tips and Tricks for Using the Airfryer

1. Preheat your airfryer before adding food. This will help cook the food more evenly.

2. Cut food into smaller pieces so it cooks faster and more evenly.

3. Use an oil spray to help ensure food doesn't stick to the basket and to help with even cooking.

4. Don't overcrowd the air fryer basket. This will also help with even cooking.

5. Shake or flip the basket halfway through cooking to ensure even cooking on all sides.

6. Some air fryers have a timer function – use this to your advantage so you don't overcook your food.

7. When in doubt, cook at a lower temperature for a longer period of time rather than at a higher temperature for a shorter period of time – this will help prevent overcooking or burnt food.

8. Know what foods work well in an air fryer and which don't before you start cooking – not all foods are suitable for air frying (e.g., wet or breaded foods may not work as well).

9. If possible, use fresh ingredients rather than frozen when air frying as frozen ingredients can release moisture and affect how well the food cooks.

10. Have fun experimenting with new recipes specifically made for air fryers – there are tons of recipes in this book for you to try!

Cheddar Eggs

Prep time: 5 minutes
Cook time: 15 minutes
Serves 2

Ingredients :

- 4 large eggs
- 2 tablespoons unsalted butter, melted
- 120 ml shredded sharp Cheddar cheese

Preparation Instructions :

1. Crack eggs into a round baking dish and whisk. Place dish into the air fryer basket.
2. Adjust the temperature to 204ºC and set the timer for 10 minutes.
3. After 5 minutes, stir the eggs and add the butter and cheese. Let cook 3 more minutes and stir again.
4. Allow eggs to finish cooking an additional 2 minutes or remove if they are to your desired liking.
5. Use a fork to fluff. Serve warm.

Berry Muffins

Prep time: 15 minutes
Cook time: 12 to 17 minutes
Makes 8

Ingredients :

muffins

- 315 ml plus 1 tablespoon plain flour, divided
- 60 ml granulated sugar
- 2 tablespoons light brown sugar
- 2 teaspoons baking powder
- 2 eggs
- 160 ml whole milk
- 80 ml neutral oil
- 235 ml mixed fresh berries

Preparation Instructions :

1. In a medium bowl, stir together 315 ml of flour, the granulated sugar, brown sugar, and baking powder until mixed well.
2. In a small bowl, whisk the eggs, milk, and oil until combined. Stir the egg mixture into the dry ingredients just until combined.
3. In another small bowl, toss the mixed berries with the remaining 1 tablespoon of flour until coated. Gently stir the berries into the batter.
4. Double up 16 foil muffin cups to make 8 cups.
5. Insert the crisper plate into the basket and the basket into the unit. Preheat the unit by selecting BAKE, setting the temperature to 156ºC, and setting the time to 3 minutes. Select START/STOP to begin.
6. Once the unit is preheated, place 1 L into the basket and fill each three-quarters full with the batter.
7. Select BAKE, set the temperature to 156ºC, and set the time for 17 minutes. Select START/STOP to begin.
8. After about 12 minutes, check the muffins. If they spring back when lightly touched with your finger, they are done. If not, resume cooking.
9. When the cooking is done, transfer the muffins to a wire rack to cool.
10. Repeat steps 6, 7, and 8 with the remaining muffin cups and batter.
11. Let the muffins cool for 10 minutes before serving.

Egg in a Hole

Prep time: 5 minutes
Cook time: 5 minutes
Serves 1

Ingredients :

- 1 slice bread
- 1 teaspoon butter, softened
- 1 egg
- Salt and pepper, to taste
- 1 tablespoon shredded Cheddar cheese
- 2 teaspoons diced ham

Preparation Instructions :

1. Preheat the air fryer to 166ºC. Place a baking dish in the air fryer basket.
2. On a flat work surface, cut a hole in the center of the bread slice with a 2½-inch-diameter biscuit cutter.
3. Spread the butter evenly on each side of the bread slice and transfer to the baking dish.
4. Crack the egg into the hole and season as desired with salt and pepper. Scatter the shredded cheese and diced ham on top.
5. Bake in the preheated air fryer for 5 minutes until the bread is lightly browned and the egg is cooked to your preference.
6. Remove from the basket and serve hot.

Scotch Eggs

Prep time: 10 minutes
Cook time: 20 to 25 minutes
Serves 4

Ingredients :

- 2 tablespoons flour, plus extra for coating
- 450 g sausage meat
- 4 hard-boiled eggs, peeled
- 1 raw egg
- 1 tablespoon water
- Oil for misting or cooking spray
- Crumb Coating:
- 180 ml panko bread crumbs
- 180 ml flour

Preparation Instructions :

1. Combine flour with sausage meat and mix thoroughly.
2. Divide into 4 equal portions and mold each around a hard-boiled egg so the sausage completely covers the egg.
3. In a small bowl, beat together the raw egg and water.
4. Dip sausage-covered eggs in the remaining flour, then the egg mixture, then roll in the crumb coating.
5. Air fry at 182ºC for 10 minutes. Spray eggs, turn, and spray other side.
6. Continue cooking for another 10 to 15 minutes or until sausage is well done.

Denver Omelette

Prep time: 5 minutes
Cook time: 8 minutes
Serves 1

Ingredients :

- 2 large eggs
- 60 ml unsweetened, unflavoured almond milk
- ¼ teaspoon fine sea salt
- ⅛ teaspoon ground black pepper
- 60 ml diced ham (omit for vegetarian)
- 60 ml diced green and red peppers
- 2 tablespoons diced spring onions, plus more for garnish
- 60 ml shredded Cheddar cheese (about 30 g) (omit for dairy-free)
- Quartered cherry tomatoes, for serving (optional)

Preparation Instructions :

1. Preheat the air fryer to 176ºC. Grease a

cake pan and set aside.

2. In a small bowl, use a fork to whisk together the eggs, almond milk, salt, and pepper. Add the ham, peppers, and spring onions. Pour the mixture into the greased pan. Add the cheese on top (if using).

3. Place the pan in the basket of the air fryer. Bake for 8 minutes, or until the eggs are cooked to your liking.

4. Loosen the omelette from the sides of the pan with a spatula and place it on a serving plate. Garnish with spring onions and serve with cherry tomatoes, if desired. Best served fresh.

Oat and Chia Porridge

Prep time: 10 minutes
Cook time: 5 minutes
Serves 4

Ingredients :

- 2 tablespoons peanut butter
- 4 tablespoons honey
- 1 tablespoon butter, melted
- 1 L milk
- 475 ml oats
- 235 ml chia seeds

Preparation Instructions :

1. Preheat the air fryer to 200°C.
2. Put the peanut butter, honey, butter, and milk in a bowl and stir to mix. Add the oats and chia seeds and stir.
3. Transfer the mixture to a bowl and bake in the air fryer for 5 minutes. Give another stir before serving.

Portobello Eggs Benedict

Prep time: 10 minutes
Cook time: 10 to 14 minutes
Serves 2

Ingredients :

- 1 tablespoon olive oil
- 2 cloves garlic, minced
- ¼ teaspoon dried thyme
- 2 portobello mushrooms, stems removed and gills scraped out
- 2 plum tomatoes, halved lengthwise
- Salt and freshly ground black pepper, to taste
- 2 large eggs
- 2 tablespoons grated Pecorino Romano cheese
- 1 tablespoon chopped fresh parsley, for garnish
- 1 teaspoon truffle oil (optional)

Preparation Instructions :

1. Preheat the air fryer to 204°C.
2. In a small bowl, combine the olive oil, garlic, and thyme. Brush the mixture over the mushrooms and tomatoes until thoroughly coated. Season to taste with salt and freshly ground black pepper.
3. Arrange the vegetables, cut side up, in the air fryer basket. Crack an egg into the center of each mushroom and sprinkle with cheese. Air fry for 10 to 14 minutes until the vegetables are tender and the whites are firm. When cool enough to handle, coarsely chop the tomatoes and place on top of the eggs. Scatter parsley on top and drizzle with truffle oil, if desired, just before serving.

Meritage Eggs

Prep time: 5 minutes
Cook time: 8 minutes
Serves 2

Ingredients :

- 2 teaspoons unsalted butter (or coconut oil for dairy-free), for greasing the ramekins
- 4 large eggs
- 2 teaspoons chopped fresh thyme
- ½ teaspoon fine sea salt
- ¼ teaspoon ground black pepper
- 2 tablespoons double cream (or unsweetened, unflavoured almond milk for dairy-free)
- 3 tablespoons finely grated Parmesan cheese (or chive cream cheese style spread, softened, for dairy-free)
- Fresh thyme leaves, for garnish (optional)

Preparation Instructions :

1. Preheat the air fryer to 204ºC. Grease two (110 g) ramekins with the butter.
2. Crack 2 eggs into each ramekin and divide the thyme, salt, and pepper between the ramekins. Pour 1 tablespoon of the heavy cream into each ramekin. Sprinkle each ramekin with 1½ tablespoons of the Parmesan cheese.
3. Place the ramekins in the air fryer and bake for 8 minutes for soft-cooked yolks (longer if you desire a harder yolk).
4. Garnish with a sprinkle of ground black pepper and thyme leaves, if desired. Best served fresh.

Tomato and Cheddar Rolls

Prep time: 30 minutes
Cook time: 25 minutes
Makes 12 rolls

Ingredients :

- 4 plum tomatoes
- ½ clove garlic, minced
- 1 tablespoon olive oil
- ¼ teaspoon dried thyme
- Salt and freshly ground black pepper, to taste
- 1 L plain flour
- 1 teaspoon active dry yeast
- 2 teaspoons sugar
- 2 teaspoons salt
- 1 tablespoon olive oil
- 235 ml grated Cheddar cheese, plus more for sprinkling at the end
- 350 ml water

Preparation Instructions :

1. Cut the tomatoes in half, remove the seeds with your fingers and transfer to a bowl. Add the garlic, olive oil, dried thyme, salt and freshly ground black pepper and toss well.
2. Preheat the air fryer to 200ºC.
3. Place the tomatoes, cut side up in the air fryer basket and air fry for 10 minutes. The tomatoes should just start to brown. Shake the basket to redistribute the tomatoes, and air fry for another 5 to 10 minutes at 166ºC until the tomatoes are no longer juicy. Let the tomatoes cool and then rough chop them.
4. Combine the flour, yeast, sugar and salt in the bowl of a stand mixer. Add the olive oil, chopped roasted tomatoes and Cheddar cheese to the flour mixture and start to mix using the dough hook attachment. As you're mixing, add 300

ml of the water, mixing until the dough comes together. Continue to knead the dough with the dough hook for another 10 minutes, adding enough water to the dough to get it to the right consistency.

5. Transfer the dough to an oiled bowl, cover with a clean kitchen towel and let it rest and rise until it has doubled in volume, about 1 to 2 hours. Then, divide the dough into 12 equal portions. Roll each portion of dough into a ball. Lightly coat each dough ball with oil and let the dough balls rest and rise a second time, covered lightly with plastic wrap for 45 minutes. (Alternately, you can place the rolls in the refrigerator overnight and take them out 2 hours before you bake them.)

6. Preheat the air fryer to 182°C.

7. Spray the dough balls and the air fryer basket with a little olive oil. Place three rolls at a time in the basket and bake for 10 minutes. Add a little grated Cheddar cheese on top of the rolls for the last 2 minutes of air frying for an attractive finish.

Easy Buttermilk Biscuits

Prep time: 5 minutes
Cook time: 18 minutes
Makes 16 biscuits

Ingredients :

- 600 ml plain flour
- 1 tablespoon baking powder
- 1 teaspoon coarse or flaky salt
- 1 teaspoon sugar
- ½ teaspoon baking soda
- 8 tablespoons (1 stick) unsalted butter, at room temperature
- 235 ml buttermilk, chilled

Preparation Instructions :

1. Stir together the flour, baking powder, salt,

sugar, and baking powder in a large bowl.

2. Add the butter and stir to mix well. Pour in the buttermilk and stir with a rubber spatula just until incorporated.

3. Place the dough onto a lightly floured surface and roll the dough out to a disk, ½ inch thick. Cut out the biscuits with a 2-inch round cutter and re-roll any scraps until you have 16 biscuits.

4. Preheat the air fryer to 164°C.

5. Working in batches, arrange the biscuits in the air fryer basket in a single layer. Bake for about 18 minutes until the biscuits are golden brown.

6. Remove from the basket to a plate and repeat with the remaining biscuits.

7. Serve hot.

Baked Peach Oatmeal

Prep time: 5 minutes
Cook time: 30 minutes
Serves 6

Ingredients :

- Olive oil cooking spray
- 475 ml certified gluten-free rolled oats
- 475 ml unsweetened almond milk
- 60 ml honey, plus more for drizzling (optional)
- 120 ml non-fat plain Greek yoghurt
- 1 teaspoon vanilla extract
- ½ teaspoon ground cinnamon
- ¼ teaspoon salt
- 350 ml diced peaches, divided, plus more for serving (optional)

Preparation Instructions :

1. Preheat the air fryer to 192°C. Lightly coat the inside of a 6-inch cake pan with olive oil cooking spray.

2. In a large bowl, mix together the oats, almond milk, honey, yoghurt, vanilla,

cinnamon, and salt until well combined.

3. Fold in 180 ml peaches and then pour the mixture into the prepared cake pan.

4. Sprinkle the remaining peaches across the top of the oatmeal mixture. Bake in the air fryer for 30 minutes.

5. Allow to set and cool for 5 minutes before serving with additional fresh fruit and honey for drizzling, if desired.

Quick and Easy Blueberry Muffins

Prep time: 10 minutes
Cook time: 12 minutes
Makes 8 muffins

Ingredients :

- 315 ml flour
- 120 ml sugar
- 2 teaspoons baking powder
- ¼ teaspoon salt
- 80 ml rapeseed oil
- 1 egg
- 120 ml milk
- 160 ml blueberries, fresh or frozen and thawed

Preparation Instructions :

1. Preheat the air fryer to 166°C.

2. In a medium bowl, stir together flour, sugar, baking powder, and salt.

3. In a separate bowl, combine oil, egg, and milk and mix well.

4. Add egg mixture to dry ingredients and stir just until moistened.

5. Gently stir in the blueberries.

6. Spoon batter evenly into parchment paper-lined muffin cups.

7. Put 4 muffin cups in air fryer basket and bake for 12 minutes or until tops spring back when touched lightly.

8. Repeat previous step to bake remaining muffins.

9. Serve immediately.

Bacon-and-Eggs Avocado

Prep time: 5 minutes
Cook time: 17 minutes
Serves 1

Ingredients :

- 1 large egg
- 1 avocado, halved, peeled, and pitted
- 2 slices bacon
- Fresh parsley, for serving (optional)
- Sea salt flakes, for garnish (optional)

Preparation Instructions :

1. Spray the air fryer basket with avocado oil. Preheat the air fryer to 160°C. Fill a small bowl with cool water.

2. Soft-boil the egg: Place the egg in the air fryer basket. Air fry for 6 minutes for a soft yolk or 7 minutes for a cooked yolk. Transfer the egg to the bowl of cool water and let sit for 2 minutes. Peel and set aside.

3. Use a spoon to carve out extra space in the center of the avocado halves until the cavities are big enough to fit the soft-boiled egg. Place the soft-boiled egg in the center of one half of the avocado and replace the other half of the avocado on top, so the avocado appears whole on the outside.

4. Starting at one end of the avocado, wrap the bacon around the avocado to completely cover it. Use toothpicks to hold the bacon in place.

5. Place the bacon-wrapped avocado in the air fryer basket and air fry for 5 minutes. Flip the avocado over and air fry for another 5 minutes, or until the bacon is cooked to your liking. Serve on a bed of fresh parsley, if desired, and sprinkle with salt flakes, if desired.

6. Best served fresh. Store extras in an airtight container in the fridge for up to 4 days. Reheat in a preheated 160°C air fryer for 4 minutes, or until heated through.

Turkey Sausage Breakfast Pizza

Prep time: 15 minutes
Cook time: 24 minutes
Serves 2

Ingredients :

- 4 large eggs, divided
- 1 tablespoon water
- ½ teaspoon garlic powder
- ½ teaspoon onion granules
- ½ teaspoon dried oregano
- 2 tablespoons coconut flour
- 3 tablespoons grated Parmesan cheese
- 120 ml shredded low-moisture Mozzarella or other melting cheese
- 1 link cooked turkey sausage, chopped (about 60 g)
- 2 sun-dried tomatoes, finely chopped
- 2 spring onions, thinly sliced

Preparation Instructions :

1. Preheat the air fryer to 204°C. Line a cake pan with parchment paper and lightly coat the paper with olive oil.
2. In a large bowl, whisk 2 of the eggs with the water, garlic powder, onion granules, and dried oregano. Add the coconut flour, breaking up any lumps with your hands as you add it to the bowl. Stir the coconut flour into the egg mixture, mixing until smooth. Stir in the Parmesan cheese. Allow the mixture to rest for a few minutes until thick and dough-like.
3. Transfer the mixture to the prepared pan. Use a spatula to spread it evenly and slightly up the sides of the pan. Air fry until the crust is set but still light in color, about 10 minutes. Top with the cheeses, sausage, and sun-dried tomatoes.
4. Break the remaining 2 eggs into a small bowl, then slide them onto the pizza. Return the pizza to the air fryer. Air fry 10 to 14 minutes until the egg whites are set and the yolks are the desired doneness. Top with the scallions and allow to rest for 5 minutes before serving.

Cheesy Bell Pepper Eggs

Prep time: 10 minutes
Cook time: 15 minutes
Serves 4

Ingredients :

- 4 medium green peppers
- 85 g cooked ham, chopped
- ¼ medium onion, peeled and chopped
- 8 large eggs
- 235 ml mild Cheddar cheese

Preparation Instructions :

1. Cut the tops off each pepper. Remove the seeds and the white membranes with a small knife. Place ham and onion into each pepper.
2. Crack 2 eggs into each pepper. Top with 60 ml cheese per pepper. Place into the air fryer basket.
3. Adjust the temperature to 200°C and air fry for 15 minutes.
4. When fully cooked, peppers will be tender and eggs will be firm. Serve immediately.

Puffed Egg Tarts

Prep time: 10 minutes
Cook time: 42 minutes
Makes 4 tarts

Ingredients :

- Oil, for spraying
- Plain flour, for dusting
- 1 (340 g) sheet frozen puff pastry, thawed
- 180 ml shredded Cheddar cheese, divided
- 4 large eggs
- 2 teaspoons chopped fresh parsley
- Salt and freshly ground black pepper, to taste

Preparation Instructions :

1. Preheat the air fryer to 200°C.
2. Line the air fryer basket with parchment and spray lightly with oil.
3. Lightly dust your work surface with flour. Unfold the puff pastry and cut it into 4 equal squares.
4. Place 2 squares in the prepared basket. Cook for 10 minutes. Remove the basket.
5. Press the centre of each tart shell with a spoon to make an indentation. Sprinkle 3 tablespoons of cheese into each indentation and crack 1 egg into the centre of each tart shell. Cook for another 7 to 11 minutes, or until the eggs are cooked to your desired doneness.
6. Repeat with the remaining puff pastry squares, cheese, and eggs. Sprinkle evenly with the parsley, and season with salt and black pepper.
7. Serve immediately.

Chinese-Inspired Spareribs

Prep time: 30 minutes
Cook time: 8 minutes
Serves 4

Ingredients :

- Oil, for spraying
- 340 g boneless pork spareribs, cut into 3-inch-long pieces
- 235 ml soy sauce
- 180 ml sugar
- 120 ml beef or chicken stock
- 60 ml honey
- 2 tablespoons minced garlic
- 1 teaspoon ground ginger
- 2 drops red food colouring (optional)

Preparation Instructions :

1. Line the air fryer basket with parchment and spray lightly with oil.
2. Combine the ribs, soy sauce, sugar, beef stock, honey, garlic, ginger, and food colouring (if using) in a large zip-top plastic bag, seal, and shake well until completely coated.
3. Refrigerate for at least 30 minutes.
4. Place the ribs in the prepared basket. Air fry at 192°C for 8 minutes, or until the internal temperature reaches 74°C.

Beef Jerky

Prep time: 30 minutes
Cook time: 2 hours
Serves 8

Ingredients :

- Oil, for spraying
- 450 g silverside steak, cut into thin, short slices
- 60 ml soy sauce
- 3 tablespoons packed light brown sugar
- 1 tablespoon minced garlic
- 1 teaspoon ground ginger
- 1 tablespoon water

Preparation Instructions :

1. Line the air fryer basket with parchment and spray lightly with oil.
2. Place the steak, soy sauce, brown sugar, garlic, ginger, and water in a zip-top plastic bag, seal, and shake well until evenly coated.
3. Refrigerate for 30 minutes.
4. Place the steak in the prepared basket in a single layer. You may need to work in batches, depending on the size of your air fryer.
5. Air fry at 82°C for at least 2 hours. Add more time if you like your jerky a bit tougher.

Cajun Shrimp

Prep time: 15 minutes
Cook time: 9 minutes
Serves 4

Ingredients :

- Oil, for spraying
- 450 g jumbo raw shrimp, peeled and deveined
- 1 tablespoon Cajun seasoning
- 170 g cooked kielbasa, cut into thick slices
- ½ medium courgette, cut into ¼-inch-thick slices
- ½ medium yellow squash or butternut squash, cut into ¼-inch-thick slices
- 1 green pepper, seeded and cut into 1-inch pieces
- 2 tablespoons olive oil
- ½ teaspoon salt

Preparation Instructions :

1. Preheat the air fryer to 204°C.
2. Line the air fryer basket with parchment and spray lightly with oil.
3. In a large bowl, toss together the shrimp and Cajun seasoning. Add the kielbasa, courgette, squash, pepper, olive oil, and salt and mix well.
4. Transfer the mixture to the prepared basket, taking care not to overcrowd. You may need to work in batches, depending on the size of your air fryer.
5. Cook for 9 minutes, shaking and stirring every 3 minutes.
6. Serve immediately.

Churro Bites

Prep time: 5 minutes
Cook time: 6 minutes
Makes 36 bites

Ingredients :

- Oil, for spraying
- 1 (500 g) package frozen puffed pastry, thawed
- 235 ml granulated sugar
- 1 tablespoon ground cinnamon
- 120 ml icing sugar
- 1 tablespoon milk

Preparation Instructions :

1. Preheat the air fryer to 204°C.
2. Line the air fryer basket with parchment and spray lightly with oil. Unfold the puff pastry onto a clean work surface.
3. Using a sharp knife, cut the dough into 36 bite-size pieces. Place the dough pieces in one layer in the prepared basket, taking care not to let the pieces touch or overlap.
4. Cook for 3 minutes, flip, and cook for another 3 minutes, or until puffed and golden.
5. In a small bowl, mix together the granulated sugar and cinnamon.
6. In another small bowl, whisk together the icing sugar and milk. Dredge the bites in the cinnamon-sugar mixture until evenly coated.
7. Serve with the icing on the side for dipping.

Avocado and Egg Burrito

Prep time: 10 minutes
Cook time: 3 to 5 minutes
Serves 4

Ingredients :

- 2 hard-boiled egg whites, chopped
- 1 hard-boiled egg, chopped
- 1 avocado, peeled, pitted, and chopped
- 1 red pepper, chopped
- 3 tablespoons low-salt salsa, plus additional for serving (optional)
- 1 (34 g) slice low-salt, low-fat processed cheese, torn into pieces
- 4 low-salt wholemeal flour tortillas

Preparation Instructions :

1. In a medium bowl, thoroughly mix the egg whites, egg, avocado, red pepper, salsa, and cheese.
2. Place the tortillas on a work surface and evenly divide the filling among them.
3. Fold in the edges and roll up. Secure the burritos with toothpicks if necessary.
4. Put the burritos in the air fryer basket. Air fry at 200°C for 3 to 5 minutes, or until the burritos are light golden brown and crisp.
5. Serve with more salsa (if using).

Cheesy Roasted Sweet Potatoes

Prep time: 7 minutes
Cook time: 18 to 23 minutes
Serves 4

Ingredients :

- 2 large sweet potatoes, peeled and sliced
- 1 teaspoon olive oil
- 1 tablespoon white balsamic vinegar
- 1 teaspoon dried thyme
- 60 ml grated Parmesan cheese

Preparation Instructions :

In a large bowl, drizzle the sweet potato slices with the olive oil and toss. Sprinkle with the balsamic vinegar and thyme and toss again. Sprinkle the potatoes with the Parmesan cheese and toss to coat. Roast the slices, in batches, in the air fryer basket at 204°C for 18 to 23 minutes, tossing the sweet potato slices in the basket once during cooking, until tender. Repeat with the remaining sweet potato slices. Serve immediately.

Pork Burgers with Red Cabbage Salad

Prep time: 20 minutes
Cook time: 7 to 9 minutes
Serves 4

Ingredients :

- 120 ml Greek yoghurt
- 2 tablespoons low-salt mustard, divided
- 1 tablespoon lemon juice
- 60 ml sliced red cabbage
- 60 ml grated carrots
- 450 g lean minced pork
- ½ teaspoon paprika
- 235 ml mixed baby lettuce greens
- 2 small tomatoes, sliced
- 8 small low-salt wholemeal sandwich buns, cut in half

Preparation Instructions :

1. In a large bowl, drizzle the sweet potato slices with the olive oil and toss.
2. Sprinkle with the balsamic vinegar and thyme and toss again.
3. Sprinkle the potatoes with the Parmesan cheese and toss to coat.
4. Roast the slices, in batches, in the air fryer basket at 204°C for 18 to 23 minutes, tossing the sweet potato slices in the basket once during cooking, until tender.
5. Repeat with the remaining sweet potato slices.
6. Serve immediately.

Fried Green Tomatoes

Prep time: 15 minutes
Cook time: 6 to 8 minutes
Serves 4

Ingredients :

- 4 medium green tomatoes
- 80 ml plain flour
- 2 egg whites
- 60 ml almond milk
- 235 ml ground almonds
- 120 ml panko breadcrumbs
- 2 teaspoons olive oil
- 1 teaspoon paprika
- 1 clove garlic, minced

Preparation Instructions :

1. Rinse the tomatoes and pat dry.
2. Cut the tomatoes into ½-inch slices, discarding the thinner ends.
3. Put the flour on a plate.
4. In a shallow bowl, beat the egg whites with the almond milk until frothy.
5. And on another plate, combine the almonds, breadcrumbs, olive oil, paprika, and garlic and mix well.
6. Dip the tomato slices into the flour, then into the egg white mixture, then into the almond mixture to coat.
7. Place four of the coated tomato slices in the air fryer basket. Air fry at 204°C for 6 to 8 minutes or until the tomato coating is crisp and golden brown.
8. Repeat with remaining tomato slices and serve immediately.

Old Bay Tilapia

Prep time: 15 minutes
Cook time: 6 minutes
Serves 4

Ingredients :

- Oil, for spraying
- 235 ml panko breadcrumbs
- 2 tablespoons Old Bay or all-purpose seasoning
- 2 teaspoons granulated garlic
- 1 teaspoon onion powder
- ½ teaspoon salt
- ¼ teaspoon freshly ground black pepper
- 1 large egg
- 4 tilapia fillets

Preparation Instructions :

1. Preheat the air fryer to 204°C.
2. Line the air fryer basket with parchment and spray lightly with oil.
3. In a shallow bowl, mix together the breadcrumbs, seasoning, garlic, onion powder, salt, and black pepper.
4. In a small bowl, whisk the egg.
5. Coat the tilapia in the egg, then dredge in the bread crumb mixture until completely coated.
6. Place the tilapia in the prepared basket. You may need to work in batches, depending on the size of your air fryer.
7. Spray lightly with oil. Cook for 4 to 6 minutes, depending on the thickness of the fillets, until the internal temperature reaches 64°C.
8. Serve immediately.

Garlicky Knots with Parsley

Prep time: 10 minutes
Cook time: 10 minutes
Makes 8 knots

Ingredients :

- 1 teaspoon dried parsley
- 60 ml melted butter
- 2 teaspoons garlic powder
- 1 (312 g) tube refrigerated French bread dough, cut into 8 slices

Preparation Instructions :

1. Preheat the air fryer to 176°C.
2. Combine the parsley, butter, and garlic powder in a bowl. Stir to mix well.
3. Place the French bread dough slices on a clean work surface, then roll each slice into a 6-inch-long rope.
4. Tie the ropes into knots and arrange them on a plate.
5. Brush the knots with butter mixture. Transfer the knots into the air fryer.
6. You need to work in batches to avoid overcrowding. Air fry for 5 minutes or until the knots are golden brown. Flip the knots halfway through the cooking time.
7. Serve immediately.

Mushroom and Green Bean Casserole

Prep time: 10 minutes
Cook time: 15 minutes
Serves 4

Ingredients :

- 4 tablespoons unsalted butter
- 60 ml diced brown onion
- 120 ml chopped white mushrooms
- 120 ml double cream
- 30 g full fat soft white cheese
- 120 ml chicken broth
- ¼ teaspoon xanthan gum
- 450 g fresh green beans, edges trimmed
- 14 g pork crackling, finely ground

Preparation Instructions :

1. In a medium skillet over medium heat, melt the butter.
2. Sauté the onion and mushrooms until they become soft and fragrant, about 3 to 5 minutes. Add the double cream, soft white cheese, and broth to the pan. Whisk until smooth. Bring to a boil and then reduce to a simmer. Sprinkle the xanthan gum into the pan and remove from heat.
3. Preheat the air fryer to 160°C.
4. Chop the green beans into 2-inch pieces and place into a baking dish.
5. Pour the sauce mixture over them and stir until coated. Top the dish with minced pork crackling. Put into the air fryer basket and bake for 15 minutes.
6. Top will be golden and green beans fork-tender when fully cooked.

Lush Snack Mix

Prep time: 10 minutes
Cook time: 10 minutes
Serves 10

Ingredients :

- 120 ml honey
- 3 tablespoons butter, melted
- 1 teaspoon salt
- 475 ml sesame sticks
- 475 ml pumpkin seeds
- 475 ml granola
- 235 ml cashews
- 475 ml crispy corn puff cereal
- 475 ml mini pretzel crisps

Preparation Instructions :

1. In a bowl, combine the honey, butter, and salt.
2. In another bowl, mix the sesame sticks, pumpkin seeds, granola, cashews, corn puff cereal, and pretzel crisps.
3. Combine the contents of the two bowls.
4. Preheat the air fryer to 188°C. Put the mixture in the air fryer basket and air fry for 10 to 12 minutes to toast the snack mixture, shaking the basket frequently. Do this in two batches.
5. Put the snack mix on a cookie sheet and allow it to cool fully.
6. Serve immediately.

Teriyaki Shrimp Skewers

Prep time: 10 minutes
Cook time: 6 minutes
Makes 12 skewered shrimp

Ingredients :

- 1½ tablespoons mirin
- 1½ teaspoons ginger paste
- 1½ tablespoons soy sauce
- 12 large shrimp, peeled and deveined
- 1 large egg
- 180 ml panko breadcrumbs
- Cooking spray

Preparation Instructions :

1. Combine the mirin, ginger paste, and soy sauce in a large bowl. Stir to mix well.
2. Dunk the shrimp in the bowl of mirin mixture, then wrap the bowl in plastic and refrigerate for 1 hour to marinate.
3. Preheat the air fryer to 204°C. Spritz the air fryer basket with cooking spray.
4. Run twelve 4-inch skewers through each shrimp.
5. Whisk the egg in the bowl of marinade to combine well. Pour the breadcrumbs on a plate.
6. Dredge the shrimp skewers in the egg mixture, then shake the excess off and roll over the breadcrumbs to coat well.
7. Arrange the shrimp skewers in the preheated air fryer and spritz with cooking spray. You need to work in batches to avoid overcrowding.
8. Air fry for 6 minutes or until the shrimp are opaque and firm. Flip the shrimp skewers halfway through. Serve immediately.

Eggnog Bread

Prep time: 10 minutes
Cook time: 18 minutes
Serves 6 to 8

Ingredients :

- 235 ml flour, plus more for dusting
- 60 ml sugar
- 1 teaspoon baking powder
- ¼ teaspoon salt
- ¼ teaspoon nutmeg
- 120 ml eggnog
- 1 egg yolk
- 1 tablespoon plus 1 teaspoon butter, melted
- 60 ml pecans
- 60 ml chopped candied fruit (cherries, pineapple, or mixed fruits)
- Cooking spray

Preparation Instructions :

1. Preheat the air fryer to 182ºC.
2. In a medium bowl, stir together the flour, sugar, baking powder, salt, and nutmeg.
3. Add eggnog, egg yolk, and butter. Mix well but do not beat.
4. Stir in nuts and fruit.
5. Spray a baking pan with cooking spray and dust with flour. Spread batter into prepared pan and bake for 18 minutes or until top is dark golden brown and bread starts to pull away from sides of pan.
6. Serve immediately.

Simple Cheesy Shrimps

Prep time: 10 minutes
Cook time: 16 minutes
Serves 4 to 6

Ingredients :

- 160 ml grated Parmesan cheese
- 4 minced garlic cloves
- 1 teaspoon onion powder
- ½ teaspoon oregano
- 1 teaspoon basil
- 1 teaspoon ground black pepper
- 2 tablespoons olive oil
- 900 g cooked large shrimps, peeled and deveined
- Lemon wedges, for topping
- Cooking spray

Preparation Instructions :

1. Preheat the air fryer to 176ºC. Spritz the air fryer basket with cooking spray.
2. Combine all the ingredients, except for the shrimps, in a large bowl. Stir to mix well. Dunk the shrimps in the mixture and toss to coat well. Shake the excess off.
3. Arrange the shrimps in the preheated air fryer. Air fry for 8 minutes or until opaque. Flip the shrimps halfway through. You may need to work in batches to avoid overcrowding.
4. Transfer the cooked shrimps on a large plate and squeeze the lemon wedges over before serving.

Fried Dill Pickles with Buttermilk Dressing

Prep time: 45 minutes
Cook time: 8 minutes
Serves 6 to 8

Ingredients :

- Buttermilk Dressing:
- 60 ml buttermilk
- 60 ml chopped spring onions
- 180 ml mayonnaise
- 120 ml sour cream
- ½ teaspoon cayenne pepper
- ½ teaspoon onion powder
- ½ teaspoon garlic powder
- 1 tablespoon chopped chives
- 2 tablespoons chopped fresh dill
- Rock salt and ground black pepper, to taste
- Fried Dill Pickles:
- 180 ml plain flour
- 1 (900 g) jar kosher dill pickles, cut into 4 spears, drained
- 600 ml panko breadcrumbs
- 2 eggs, beaten with 2 tablespoons water
- Rock salt and ground black pepper, to taste
- Cooking spray

Preparation Instructions :

1. Preheat the air fryer to 204ºC.
2. Combine the ingredients for the dressing in a bowl. Stir to mix well. Wrap the bowl in plastic and refrigerate for 30 minutes or until ready to serve.
3. Pour the flour in a bowl and sprinkle with salt and ground black pepper.
4. Stir to mix well. Put the breadcrumbs in a separate bowl.
5. Pour the beaten eggs in a third bowl. Dredge the pickle spears in the flour, then into the eggs, and then into the panko to coat well. Shake the excess off.
6. Arrange the pickle spears in a single layer in the preheated air fryer and spritz with cooking spray. Air fry for 8 minutes. Flip the pickle spears halfway through.
7. Serve the pickle spears with buttermilk dressing.

Whole Chicken Roast

Prep time: 10 minutes
Cook time: 1 hour
Serves 6

Ingredients :

- 1 teaspoon salt
- 1 teaspoon Italian seasoning
- ½ teaspoon freshly ground black pepper
- ½ teaspoon paprika
- ½ teaspoon garlic powder
- ½ teaspoon onion powder
- 2 tablespoons olive oil, plus more as needed
- 1 (1.8 kg) small chicken

Preparation Instructions :

1. Preheat the air fryer to 182ºC.
2. Grease the air fryer basket lightly with olive oil. In a small bowl, mix the salt, Italian seasoning, pepper, paprika, garlic powder, and onion powder.
3. Remove any giblets from the chicken. Pat the chicken dry thoroughly with paper towels, including the cavity.
4. Brush the chicken all over with the olive oil and rub it with the seasoning mixture.
5. Truss the chicken or tie the legs with butcher's twine. This will make it easier to flip the chicken during cooking.
6. Put the chicken in the air fryer basket, breast-side down. Air fry for 30 minutes.
Flip the chicken over and baste it with any drippings collected in the bottom drawer of the air fryer.
7. Lightly brush the chicken with olive oil.

Air fry for 20 minutes.

8. Flip the chicken over one last time and air fry until a thermometer inserted into the thickest part of the thigh reaches at least 74°C and it's crispy and golden, 10 more minutes. Continue to cook, checking every 5 minutes until the chicken reaches the correct internal temperature.

9. Let the chicken rest for 10 minutes before carving and serving.

Classic Churros

Prep time: 35 minutes
Cook time: 10 minutes per batch
Makes 12 churros

Ingredients :

- 4 tablespoons butter
- ¼ teaspoon salt
- 120 ml water
- 120 ml plain flour
- 2 large eggs
- 2 teaspoons ground cinnamon
- 60 ml granulated white sugar
- Cooking spray

Preparation Instructions :

1. Put the butter, salt, and water in a saucepan. Bring to a boil until the butter is melted on high heat.
2. Keep stirring. Reduce the heat to medium and fold in the flour to form a dough. Keep cooking and stirring until the dough is dried out and coat the pan with a crust.
3. Turn off the heat and scrape the dough in a large bowl. Allow to cool for 15 minutes.
4. Break and whisk the eggs into the dough with a hand mixer until the dough is sanity and firm enough to shape. Scoop up 1 tablespoon of the dough and roll it into a ½-inch-diameter and 2-inch-long cylinder.

5. Repeat with remaining dough to make 12 cylinders in total. Combine the cinnamon and sugar in a large bowl and dunk the cylinders into the cinnamon mix to coat.
6. Arrange the cylinders on a plate and refrigerate for 20 minutes.
7. Preheat the air fryer to 192°C. Spritz the air fryer basket with cooking spray.
8. Place the cylinders in batches in the air fryer basket and spritz with cooking spray. Air fry for 10 minutes or until golden brown and fluffy. Flip them halfway through.
9. Serve immediately.

Simple Air Fried Crispy Brussels Sprouts

Prep time: 5 minutes
Cook time: 20 minutes
Serves 4

Ingredients :

- ¼ teaspoon salt
- ⅛ teaspoon ground black pepper
- 1 tablespoon extra-virgin olive oil
- 450 g Brussels sprouts, trimmed and halved
- Lemon wedges, for garnish

Preparation Instructions :

1. Preheat the air fryer to 176°C.
2. Combine the salt, black pepper, and olive oil in a large bowl. Stir to mix well.
3. Add the Brussels sprouts to the bowl of mixture and toss to coat well.
4. Arrange the Brussels sprouts in the preheated air fryer. Air fry for 20 minutes or until lightly browned and wilted. Shake the basket two times during the air frying.
5. Transfer the cooked Brussels sprouts to a large plate and squeeze the lemon wedges on top to serve.

Beef and Mango Skewers

Prep time: 10 minutes
Cook time: 4 to 7 minutes
Serves 4

Ingredients :

- 340 g beef sirloin tip, cut into 1-inch cubes
- 2 tablespoons balsamic vinegar
- 1 tablespoon olive oil
- 1 tablespoon honey
- ½ teaspoon dried marjoram
- Pinch of salt
- Freshly ground black pepper, to taste
- 1 mango

Preparation Instructions :

1. Preheat the air fryer to 200°C.
2. Put the beef cubes in a medium bowl and add the balsamic vinegar, olive oil, honey, marjoram, salt, and pepper. Mix well, then massage the marinade into the beef with your hands. Set aside.
3. To prepare the mango, stand it on end and cut the skin off, using a sharp knife. Then carefully cut around the oval pit to remove the flesh. Cut the mango into 1-inch cubes.
4. Thread metal skewers alternating with three beef cubes and two mango cubes.
5. Roast the skewers in the air fryer basket for 4 to 7 minutes, or until the beef is browned and at least 63°C.
6. Serve hot.

Classic Spring Rolls

Prep time: 10 minutes
Cook time: 9 minutes
Makes 16 spring rolls

Ingredients :

- 4 teaspoons toasted sesame oil
- 6 medium garlic cloves, minced or pressed
- 1 tablespoon grated peeled fresh ginger
- 475 ml thinly sliced shiitake mushrooms
- 1 L chopped green cabbage
- 240 ml grated carrot
- ½ teaspoon sea salt
- 16 rice paper wrappers
- Cooking oil spray (sunflower, safflower, or refined coconut)
- Gluten-free sweet and sour sauce or Thai sweet chilli sauce, for serving (optional)

Preparation Instructions :

1. Place a wok or sauté pan over medium heat until hot.
2. Add the sesame oil, garlic, ginger, mushrooms, cabbage, carrot, and salt. Cook for 3 to 4 minutes, stirring often, until the cabbage is lightly wilted. Remove the pan from the heat.
3. Gently run a rice paper under water. Lay it on a flat non-absorbent surface. Place about 60 ml of the cabbage filling in the middle. Once the wrapper is soft enough to roll, fold the bottom up over the filling, fold in the sides, and roll the wrapper all the way up. (Basically, make a tiny burrito.)
4. Repeat step 3 to make the remaining spring rolls until you have the number of spring rolls you want to cook right now

(and the amount that will fit in the air fryer basket in a single layer without them touching each other). Refrigerate any leftover filling in an airtight container for about 1 week.

5. Insert the crisper plate into the basket and the basket into the unit. Preheat the unit by selecting AIR FRY, setting the temperature to 200°C, and setting the time to 3 minutes. Select START/STOP to begin.

6. Once the unit is preheated, spray the crisper plate and the basket with cooking oil. Place the spring rolls into the basket, leaving a little room between them so they don't stick to each other. Spray the top of each spring roll with cooking oil.

7. Select AIR FRY, set the temperature to 200°C, and set the time to 9 minutes. Select START/STOP to begin.

8. When the cooking is complete, the egg rolls should be crisp-ish and lightly browned. Serve immediately, plain or with a sauce of choice.

Old Bay Chicken Wings

Prep time: 10 minutes
Cook time: 12 to 15 minutes
Serves 4

Ingredients :

- 2 tablespoons Old Bay or all-purpose seasoning
- 2 teaspoons baking powder
- 2 teaspoons salt
- 900 g chicken wings, patted dry
- Cooking spray

Preparation Instructions :

1. Preheat the air fryer to 204°C. Lightly spray the air fryer basket with cooking spray.
2. Combine the seasoning, baking powder,

and salt in a large zip-top plastic bag. Add the chicken wings, seal, and shake until the wings are thoroughly coated in the seasoning mixture.

3. Lay the chicken wings in the air fryer basket in a single layer and lightly mist with cooking spray. You may need to work in batches to avoid overcrowding.

4. Air fry for 12 to 15 minutes, flipping the wings halfway through, or until the wings are lightly browned and the internal temperature reaches at least 74°C on a meat thermometer.

5. Remove from the basket to a plate and repeat with the remaining chicken wings.

6. Serve hot.

Spicy Tortilla Chips

Prep time: 5 minutes
Cook time: 8 to 12 minutes
Serves 4

Ingredients :

- ½ teaspoon ground cumin
- ½ teaspoon paprika
- ½ teaspoon chilli powder
- ½ teaspoon salt
- Pinch cayenne pepper
- 8 (6-inch) corn tortillas, each cut into 6 wedges
- Cooking spray

Preparation Instructions :

1. Preheat the air fryer to 192°C. Lightly spritz the air fryer basket with cooking spray.
2. Stir together the cumin, paprika, chilli powder, salt, and pepper in a small bowl.
3. Working in batches, arrange the tortilla wedges in the air fryer basket in a single layer. Lightly mist them with cooking spray. Sprinkle some seasoning mixture

on top of the tortilla wedges.

4. Air fry for 4 to 6 minutes, shaking the basket halfway through, or until the chips are lightly browned and crunchy.

5. Repeat with the remaining tortilla wedges and seasoning mixture.

6. Let the tortilla chips cool for 5 minutes and serve.

Greek Potato Skins with Olives and Feta

Prep time: 5 minutes
Cook time: 45 minutes
Serves 4

Ingredients :

- 2 russet or Maris Piper potatoes
- 3 tablespoons olive oil, divided, plus more for drizzling (optional)
- 1 teaspoon rock salt, divided
- ¼ teaspoon black pepper
- 2 tablespoons fresh coriander, chopped, plus more for serving
- 60 ml Kalamata olives, diced
- 60 ml crumbled feta
- Chopped fresh parsley, for garnish (optional)

Preparation Instructions :

1. Preheat the air fryer to 192ºC.

2. Using a fork, poke 2 to 3 holes in the potatoes, then coat each with about ½ tablespoon olive oil and ½ teaspoon salt.

3. Place the potatoes into the air fryer basket and bake for 30 minutes.

4. Remove the potatoes from the air fryer, and slice in half. Using a spoon, scoop out the flesh of the potatoes, leaving a ½-inch layer of potato inside the skins, and set the skins aside.

5. In a medium bowl, combine the scooped potato middles with the remaining 2 tablespoons of olive oil, ½ teaspoon of

salt, black pepper, and coriander. Mix until well combined.

6. Divide the potato filling into the now-empty potato skins, spreading it evenly over them. Top each potato with a tablespoon each of the olives and feta.

7. Place the loaded potato skins back into the air fryer and bake for 15 minutes.

8. Serve with additional chopped coriander or parsley and a drizzle of olive oil, if desired.

Tortellini with Spicy Dipping Sauce

Prep time: 5 minutes
Cook time: 20 minutes
Serves 4

Ingredients :

- 177 ml mayonnaise
- 2 tablespoons mustard
- 1 egg
- 120 ml flour
- ½ teaspoon dried oregano
- 355 ml breadcrumbs
- 2 tablespoons olive oil
- 475 ml frozen cheese tortellini

Preparation Instructions :

1. Preheat the air fryer to 192ºC.

2. In a small bowl, combine the mayonnaise and mustard and mix well. Set aside.

3. In a shallow bowl, beat the egg. In a separate bowl, combine the flour and oregano. In another bowl, combine the breadcrumbs and olive oil, and mix well.

4. Drop the tortellini, a few at a time, into the egg, then into the flour, then into the egg again, and then into the breadcrumbs to coat. Put into the air fryer basket, cooking in batches.

5. Air fry for about 10 minutes, shaking halfway through the cooking time, or until

the tortellini are crisp and golden brown on the outside. Serve with the mayonnaise mixture.

Roasted Grape Dip

Prep time: 10 minutes
Cook time: 8 to 12 minutes
Serves 6

Ingredients :

- 475 ml seedless red grapes, rinsed and patted dry
- 1 tablespoon apple cider vinegar
- 1 tablespoon honey
- 240 ml low-fat Greek yoghurt
- 2 tablespoons semi-skimmed milk
- 2 tablespoons minced fresh basil

Preparation Instructions :

1. In the air fryer basket, sprinkle the grapes with the cider vinegar and drizzle with the honey. Toss to coat. Roast the grapes at 192°C for 8 to 12 minutes, or until shrivelled but still soft. Remove from the air fryer.
2. In a medium bowl, stir together the yoghurt and milk.
3. Gently blend in the grapes and basil. Serve immediately or cover and chill for 1 to 2 hours.

Spiralized Potato Nest with Tomato Ketchup

Prep time: 10 minutes
Cook time: 15 minutes
Serves 2

Ingredients :

- 1 large russet or Maris Piper potato (about 340 g)
- 2 tablespoons vegetable oil
- 1 tablespoon hot smoked paprika
- ½ teaspoon garlic powder
- Rock salt and freshly ground black pepper, to taste
- 120 ml canned crushed tomatoes
- 2 tablespoons apple cider vinegar
- 1 tablespoon dark brown sugar
- 1 tablespoon Worcestershire sauce
- 1 teaspoon mild hot sauce

Preparation Instructions :

1. Using a spiralizer, spiralize the potato, then place in a large colander. (If you don't have a spiralizer, cut the potato into thin ⅛-inch-thick matchsticks.) Rinse the potatoes under cold running water until the water runs clear. Spread the potatoes out on a double-thick layer of paper towels and pat completely dry.
2. In a large bowl, combine the potatoes, oil, paprika, and garlic powder. Season with salt and pepper and toss to combine. Transfer the potatoes to the air fryer and air fry at 204°C until the potatoes are browned and crisp, 15 minutes, shaking the basket halfway through.
3. Meanwhile, in a small blender, purée the tomatoes, vinegar, brown sugar, Worcestershire, and hot sauce until smooth. Pour into a small saucepan or skillet and simmer over medium heat until reduced by half, 3 to 5 minutes. Pour the homemade ketchup into a bowl and let cool.
4. Remove the spiralized potato nest from the air fryer and serve hot with the ketchup.

Soft white cheese Stuffed Jalapeño Poppers

Prep time: 12 minutes

Cook time: 6 to 8 minutes

Serves 10

Ingredients :

- 227 g soft white cheese, at room temperature
- 240 ml panko breadcrumbs, divided
- 2 tablespoons fresh parsley, minced
- 1 teaspoon chilli powder
- 10 jalapeño peppers, halved and seeded
- Cooking oil spray

Preparation Instructions :

1. In a small bowl, whisk the soft white cheese, 120 ml of panko, the parsley, and chilli powder until combined. Stuff the cheese mixture into the jalapeño halves.
2. Sprinkle the tops of the stuffed jalapeños with the remaining 120 ml of panko and press it lightly into the filling.
3. Insert the crisper plate into the basket and the basket into the unit. Preheat the unit by selecting AIR FRY, setting the temperature to 192°C, and setting the time to 3 minutes. Select START/STOP to begin.
4. Once the unit is preheated, spray the crisper plate with cooking oil. Place the poppers into the basket.
5. Select AIR FRY, set the temperature to 192°C, and set the time to 8 minutes. Select START/STOP to begin.
6. After 6 minutes, check the poppers. If they are softened and the cheese is melted, they are done. If not, resume cooking.
7. When the cooking is complete, serve warm.

Lebanese Muhammara

Prep time: 15 minutes

Cook time: 15 minutes

Serves 6

Ingredients :

- 2 large red peppers
- 60 ml plus 2 tablespoons extra-virgin olive oil
- 240 ml walnut halves
- 1 tablespoon agave nectar or honey
- 1 teaspoon fresh lemon juice
- 1 teaspoon ground cumin
- 1 teaspoon rock salt
- 1 teaspoon red pepper flakes
- Raw vegetables (such as cucumber, carrots, courgette slices, or cauliflower) or toasted pitta chips, for serving

Preparation Instructions :

1. Drizzle the peppers with 2 tablespoons of the olive oil and place in the air fryer basket. Set the air fryer to 204°C for 10 minutes.
2. Add the walnuts to the basket, arranging them around the peppers. Set the air fryer to 204°C for 5 minutes.
3. Remove the peppers, seal in a resealable plastic bag, and let rest for 5 to 10 minutes. Transfer the walnuts to a plate and set aside to cool.
4. Place the softened peppers, walnuts, agave, lemon juice, cumin, salt, and ½ teaspoon of the pepper flakes in a food processor and purée until smooth.
5. Transfer the dip to a serving bowl and make an indentation in the middle. Pour the remaining 60 ml olive oil into the indentation. Garnish the dip with the remaining ½ teaspoon pepper flakes.
6. Serve with vegetables or toasted pitta chips.

Rumaki

Prep time: 30 minutes

Cook time: 10 to 12 minutes per batch

Makes about 24 rumaki

Ingredients :

- 283 g raw chicken livers
- 1 can sliced water chestnuts, drained
- 60 ml low-salt teriyaki sauce
- 12 slices turkey bacon

Preparation Instructions :

1. Cut livers into 1½-inch pieces, trimming out tough veins as you slice.
2. Place livers, water chestnuts, and teriyaki sauce in small container with lid. If needed, add another tablespoon of teriyaki sauce to make sure livers are covered. Refrigerate for 1 hour.
3. When ready to cook, cut bacon slices in half crosswise.
4. Wrap 1 piece of liver and 1 slice of water chestnut in each bacon strip. Secure with toothpick.
5. When you have wrapped half of the livers, place them in the air fryer basket in a single layer.
6. Air fry at 200°C for 10 to 12 minutes, until liver is done, and bacon is crispy.
7. While first batch cooks, wrap the remaining livers. Repeat step 6 to cook your second batch.

Goat Cheese and Garlic Crostini

Prep time: 3 minutes

Cook time: 5 minutes

Serves 4

Ingredients :

- 1 wholemeal baguette
- 60 ml olive oil
- 2 garlic cloves, minced
- 113 g goat cheese
- 2 tablespoons fresh basil, minced

Preparation Instructions :

1. Preheat the air fryer to 192°C.
2. Cut the baguette into ½-inch-thick slices.
3. In a small bowl, mix together the olive oil and garlic, then brush it over one side of each slice of bread.
4. Place the olive-oil-coated bread in a single layer in the air fryer basket and bake for 5 minutes.
5. Meanwhile, in a small bowl, mix together the goat cheese and basil.
6. Remove the toast from the air fryer, then spread a thin layer of the goat cheese mixture over the top of each piece and serve.

Air Fryer Popcorn with Garlic Salt

Prep time: 3 minutes
Cook time: 10 minutes
Serves 2

Ingredients :

- 2 tablespoons olive oil
- 60 ml popcorn kernels
- 1 teaspoon garlic salt

Preparation Instructions :

1. Preheat the air fryer to 192ºC.
2. Tear a square of aluminium foil the size of the bottom of the air fryer and place into the air fryer.
3. Drizzle olive oil over the top of the foil, and then pour in the popcorn kernels.
4. Roast for 8 to 10 minutes, or until the popcorn stops popping.
5. Transfer the popcorn to a large bowl and sprinkle with garlic salt before serving.

Crispy Green Bean Fries with Lemon-Yoghurt Sauce

Prep time: 5 minutes
Cook time: 5 minutes
Serves 4

Ingredients :

- Green Beans:
- 1 egg
- 2 tablespoons water
- 1 tablespoon wholemeal flour
- ¼ teaspoon paprika
- ½ teaspoon garlic powder
- ½ teaspoon salt
- 60 ml wholemeal breadcrumbs
- 227 g whole green beans
- Lemon-Yoghurt Sauce:
- 120 ml non-fat plain Greek yoghurt
- 1 tablespoon lemon juice
- ¼ teaspoon salt
- ⅛ teaspoon cayenne pepper

Preparation Instructions :

Make the Green Beans:

1. Preheat the air fryer to 192ºC.
2. In a medium shallow bowl, beat together the egg and water until frothy.
3. In a separate medium shallow bowl, whisk together the flour, paprika, garlic powder, and salt, then mix in the breadcrumbs.
4. Spray the bottom of the air fryer with cooking spray.
5. Dip each green bean into the egg mixture, then into the bread crumb mixture, coating the outside with the crumbs. Place the green beans in a single layer in the bottom of the air fryer basket.
6. Fry in the air fryer for 5 minutes, or until the breading is golden brown. Make the Lemon-Yoghurt Sauce:
7. In a small bowl, combine the yoghurt, lemon juice, salt, and cayenne.
8. Serve the green bean fries alongside the lemon-yoghurt sauce as a snack or appetizer.

Roasted Pearl Onion Dip

Prep time: 5 minutes
Cook time: 12 minutes
Serves 4

Ingredients :

- 475 ml peeled pearl onions
- 3 garlic cloves
- 3 tablespoons olive oil, divided
- ½ teaspoon salt
- 240 ml non-fat plain Greek yoghurt
- 1 tablespoon lemon juice
- ¼ teaspoon black pepper
- ⅛ teaspoon red pepper flakes
- Pitta chips, vegetables, or toasted bread for serving (optional)

Preparation Instructions :

1. Preheat the air fryer to 182°C.
2. In a large bowl, combine the pearl onions and garlic with 2 tablespoons of the olive oil until the onions are well coated.
3. Pour the garlic-and-onion mixture into the air fryer basket and roast for 12 minutes.
4. Transfer the garlic and onions to a food processor. Pulse the vegetables several times, until the onions are minced but still have some chunks.
5. In a large bowl, combine the garlic and onions and the remaining 1 tablespoon of olive oil, along with the salt, yoghurt, lemon juice, black pepper, and red pepper flakes.
6. Cover and chill for 1 hour before serving with pitta chips, vegetables, or toasted bread.

Shrimp Toasts with Sesame Seeds

Prep time: 15 minutes
Cook time: 6 to 8 minutes
Serves 4 to 6

Ingredients :

- 230 g raw shrimp, peeled and deveined
- 1 egg, beaten
- 2 spring onions, chopped, plus more for garnish
- 2 tablespoons chopped fresh coriander
- 2 teaspoons grated fresh ginger
- 1 to 2 teaspoons sriracha sauce
- 1 teaspoon soy sauce
- ½ teaspoon toasted sesame oil
- 6 slices thinly sliced white sandwich bread
- 120 ml sesame seeds
- Cooking spray
- Thai chilli sauce, for serving

Preparation Instructions :

1. Preheat the air fryer to 204°C. Spritz the air fryer basket with cooking spray.
2. In a food processor, add the shrimp, egg, spring onions, coriander, ginger, sriracha sauce, soy sauce and sesame oil, and pulse until chopped finely. You'll need to stop the food processor occasionally to scrape down the sides. Transfer the shrimp mixture to a bowl.
3. On a clean work surface, cut the crusts off the sandwich bread. Using a brush, generously brush one side of each slice of bread with shrimp mixture.
4. Place the sesame seeds on a plate. Press bread slices, shrimp-side down, into sesame seeds to coat evenly. Cut each slice diagonally into quarters.
5. Spread the coated slices in a single layer in the air fryer basket.
6. Air fry in batches for 6 to 8 minutes, or until golden and crispy. Flip the bread slices halfway through. Repeat with the remaining bread slices.
7. Transfer to a plate and let cool for 5 minutes. Top with the chopped spring onions and serve warm with Thai chilli sauce.

Crunchy Basil White Beans

Prep time: 2 minutes
Cook time: 19 minutes
Serves 2

Ingredients :

- 1 (425 g) can cooked white beans
- 2 tablespoons olive oil
- 1 teaspoon fresh sage, chopped
- ¼ teaspoon garlic powder
- ¼ teaspoon salt, divided
- 1 teaspoon chopped fresh basil

Preparation Instructions :

1. Preheat the air fryer to 192°C.
2. In a medium bowl, mix together the beans, olive oil, sage, garlic, ⅛ teaspoon salt, and basil.
3. Pour the white beans into the air fryer and spread them out in a single layer.
4. Bake for 10 minutes. Stir and continue cooking for an additional 5 to 9 minutes, or until they reach your preferred level of crispiness.
5. Toss with the remaining ⅛ teaspoon salt before serving.

Five-Ingredient Falafel with Garlic-Yoghurt Sauce

Prep time: 5 minutes
Cook time: 15 minutes
Serves 4

Ingredients :

- Falafel:
- 1 (425 g) can chickpeas, drained and rinsed
- 120 ml fresh parsley
- 2 garlic cloves, minced
- ½ tablespoon ground cumin
- 1 tablespoon wholemeal flour
- Salt
- Garlic-Yoghurt Sauce:
- 240 ml non-fat plain Greek yoghurt
- 1 garlic clove, minced
- 1 tablespoon chopped fresh dill
- 2 tablespoons lemon juice

Preparation Instructions :

Make the Falafel:

1. Preheat the air fryer to 182°C.
2. Put the chickpeas into a food processor. Pulse until mostly chopped, then add the parsley, garlic, and cumin and pulse for another 1 to 2 minutes, or until the ingredients are combined and turning into a dough.
3. Add the flour. Pulse a few more times until combined. The dough will have texture, but the chickpeas should be pulsed into small bits.
4. Using clean hands, roll the dough into 8 balls of equal size, then pat the balls down a bit so they are about ½-thick disks.
5. Spray the basket of the air fryer with olive oil cooking spray, then place the falafel patties in the basket in a single layer, making sure they don't touch each other.
6. Fry in the air fryer for 15 minutes. Make the garlic-yoghurt sauce
7. In a small bowl, combine the yoghurt, garlic, dill, and lemon juice.
8. Once the falafel is done cooking and nicely browned on all sides, remove them from the air fryer and season with salt.
9. Serve hot with a side of dipping sauce.

Crispy Mozzarella Sticks

Prep time: 8 minutes
Cook time: 5 minutes
Serves 4

Ingredients :

- 120 ml plain flour
- 1 egg, beaten
- 120 ml panko breadcrumbs
- 120 ml grated Parmesan cheese
- 1 teaspoon Italian seasoning
- ½ teaspoon garlic salt
- 6 Mozzarella sticks, halved crosswise
- Olive oil spray

Preparation Instructions :

1. Put the flour in a small bowl.
2. Put the beaten egg in another small bowl.
3. In a medium bowl, stir together the panko, Parmesan cheese, Italian seasoning, and

garlic salt.

4. Roll a Mozzarella-stick half in the flour, dip it into the egg, and then roll it in the panko mixture to coat. Press the coating lightly to make sure the breadcrumbs stick to the cheese. Repeat with the remaining 11 Mozzarella sticks.

5. Insert the crisper plate into the basket and the basket into the unit. Preheat the unit by selecting AIR FRY, setting the temperature to 204°C, and setting the time to 3 minutes. Select START/STOP to begin.

6. Once the unit is preheated, spray the crisper plate with olive oil and place a parchment paper liner in the basket. Place the Mozzarella sticks into the basket and lightly spray them with olive oil.

7. Select AIR FRY, set the temperature to 204°C, and set the time to 5 minutes. Select START/STOP to begin.

8. When the cooking is complete, the Mozzarella sticks should be golden and crispy. Let the sticks stand for 1 minute before transferring them to a serving plate. Serve warm.

Sweet Potato Fries with Mayonnaise

Prep time: 5 minutes
Cook time: 20 minutes
Serves 2 to 3

Ingredients :

- 1 large sweet potato (about 450 g), scrubbed
- 1 teaspoon vegetable or rapeseed oil
- Salt, to taste
- Dipping Sauce:
- 60 ml light mayonnaise
- ½ teaspoon sriracha sauce
- 1 tablespoon spicy brown mustard
- 1 tablespoon sweet Thai chilli sauce

Preparation Instructions :

1. Preheat the air fryer to 92°C.
2. On a flat work surface, cut the sweet potato into fry-shaped strips about ¼ inch wide and ¼ inch thick. You can use a mandoline to slice the sweet potato quickly and uniformly.
3. In a medium bowl, drizzle the sweet potato strips with the oil and toss well.
4. Transfer to the air fryer basket and air fry for 10 minutes, shaking the basket twice during cooking.
5. Remove the air fryer basket and sprinkle with the salt and toss to coat.
6. Increase the air fryer temperature to 204°C and air fry for an additional 10 minutes, or until the fries are crispy and tender. Shake the basket a few times during cooking.
7. Meanwhile, whisk together all the ingredients for the sauce in a small bowl.
8. Remove the sweet potato fries from the basket to a plate and serve warm alongside the dipping sauce.

Lamb Chops with Horseradish Sauce

Prep time: 30 minutes
Cook time: 13 minutes
Serves 4

Ingredients :

- Lamb:
- 4 lamb loin chops
- 2 tablespoons vegetable oil
- 1 clove garlic, minced
- ½ teaspoon coarse or flaky salt
- ½ teaspoon black pepper
- Horseradish Cream Sauce:
- 120 ml mayonnaise
- 1 tablespoon Dijon mustard
- 1 to 1½ tablespoons grated horseradish
- 2 teaspoons sugar
- Vegetable oil spray

Preparation Instructions :

1. For the lamb: Brush the lamb chops with the oil, rub with the garlic, and sprinkle with the salt and pepper. Marinate at room temperature for 30 minutes.
2. Meanwhile, for the sauce: In a medium bowl, combine the mayonnaise, mustard, horseradish, and sugar. Stir until well combined. Set aside half of the sauce for serving.
3. Spray the air fryer basket with vegetable oil spray and place the chops in the basket. Set the air fryer to 164°C for 10 minutes, turning the chops halfway through the cooking time.
4. Remove the chops from the air fryer and add to the bowl with the horseradish sauce, turning to coat with the sauce.

Place the chops back in the air fryer basket. Set the air fryer to 204°C for 3 minutes. Use a meat thermometer to ensure the meat has reached an internal temperature of 64°C (for medium-rare).
5. Serve the chops with the reserved horseradish sauce.

Pork and Tricolor Vegetables Kebabs

Prep time: 1 hour 20 minutes
Cook time: 8 minutes per batch
Serves 4

Ingredients :

- For the Pork:
- 450 g pork steak, cut in cubes
- 1 tablespoon white wine vinegar
- 3 tablespoons steak sauce or brown sauce
- 60 ml soy sauce
- 1 teaspoon powdered chili
- 1 teaspoon red chili flakes
- 2 teaspoons smoked paprika
- 1 teaspoon garlic salt
- For the Vegetable:
- 1 courgette, cut in cubes
- 1 butternut squash, deseeded and cut in cubes
- 1 red pepper, cut in cubes
- 1 green pepper, cut in cubes
- Salt and ground black pepper, to taste
- Cooking spray
- Special Equipment:
- 4 bamboo skewers, soaked in water for at least 30 minutes

Preparation Instructions :

1. Combine the ingredients for the pork in a

large bowl. Press the pork to dunk in the marinade. Wrap the bowl in plastic and refrigerate for at least an hour.

2. Preheat the air fryer to 188ºC and spritz with cooking spray.

3. Remove the pork from the marinade and run the skewers through the pork and vegetables alternately. Sprinkle with salt and pepper to taste.

4. Arrange the skewers in the preheated air fryer and spritz with cooking spray. Air fry for 8 minutes or until the pork is browned and the vegetables are lightly charred and tender. Flip the skewers halfway through. You may need to work in batches to avoid overcrowding.

5. Serve immediately.

Chuck Kebab with Rocket

Prep time: 30 minutes
Cook time: 25 minutes
Serves 4

Ingredients :

- 120 ml leeks, chopped
- 2 garlic cloves, smashed
- 900 g beef mince
- Salt, to taste
- ¼ teaspoon ground black pepper, or more to taste
- 1 teaspoon cayenne pepper
- ½ teaspoon ground sumac
- 3 saffron threads
- 2 tablespoons loosely packed fresh flat-leaf parsley leaves
- 4 tablespoons tahini sauce
- 110 g baby rocket
- 1 tomato, cut into slices

Preparation Instructions :

1. In a bowl, mix the chopped leeks, garlic, beef mince, and spices; knead with

your hands until everything is well incorporated.

2. Now, mound the beef mixture around a wooden skewer into a pointed-ended sausage.

3. Cook in the preheated air fryer at 182ºC for 25 minutes. Serve your kebab with the tahini sauce, baby rocket and tomato. Enjoy!

Mexican Pork Chops

Prep time: 5 minutes
Cook time: 15 minutes
Serves 2

Ingredients :

- ¼ teaspoon dried oregano
- 1½ teaspoons taco seasoning or fajita seasoning mix
- 2 (110 g) boneless pork chops
- 2 tablespoons unsalted butter, divided

Preparation Instructions :

1. Preheat the air fryer to 204ºC.

2. Combine the dried oregano and taco seasoning in a small bowl and rub the mixture into the pork chops. Brush the chops with 1 tablespoon butter.

3. In the air fryer, air fry the chops for 15 minutes, turning them over halfway through to air fry on the other side.

4. When the chops are a brown color, check the internal temperature has reached 64ºC and remove from the air fryer. Serve with a garnish of remaining butter.

Bone-in Pork Chops

Prep time: 5 minutes
Cook time: 10 to 12 minutes
Serves 2

Ingredients :

- 450 g bone-in pork chops
- 1 tablespoon avocado oil
- 1 teaspoon smoked paprika
- ½ teaspoon onion granules
- ¼ teaspoon cayenne pepper
- Sea salt and freshly ground black pepper, to taste

Preparation Instructions :

1. Brush the pork chops with the avocado oil. In a small dish, mix together the smoked paprika, onion granules, cayenne pepper, and salt and black pepper to taste. Sprinkle the seasonings over both sides of the pork chops.
2. Set the air fryer to 204°C. Place the chops in the air fryer basket in a single layer, working in batches if necessary. Air fry for 10 to 12 minutes, until an instant-read thermometer reads 64°C at the chops' thickest point.
3. Remove the chops from the air fryer and allow them to rest for 5 minutes before serving.

Italian Lamb Chops with Avocado Mayo

Prep time: 5 minutes
Cook time: 12 minutes
Serves 2

Ingredients :

- 2 lamp chops
- 2 teaspoons Italian herbs
- 2 avocados
- 120 ml mayonnaise
- 1 tablespoon lemon juice

Preparation Instructions :

1. Season the lamb chops with the Italian herbs, then set aside for 5 minutes.
2. Preheat the air fryer to 204°C and place the rack inside.
3. Put the chops on the rack and air fry for 12 minutes.
4. In the meantime, halve the avocados and open to remove the pits. Spoon the flesh into a blender.
5. Add the mayonnaise and lemon juice and pulse until a smooth consistency is achieved.
6. Take care when removing the chops from the air fryer, then plate up and serve with the avocado mayo.

London Broil with Herb Butter

Prep time: 30 minutes
Cook time: 20 to 25 minutes
Serves 4

Ingredients :

- 680 g bavette or skirt steak
- 60 ml olive oil
- 2 tablespoons balsamic vinegar
- 1 tablespoon Worcestershire sauce
- 4 cloves garlic, minced
- Herb Butter:
- 6 tablespoons unsalted butter, softened
- 1 tablespoon chopped fresh parsley
- ¼ teaspoon salt
- ¼ teaspoon dried ground rosemary or thyme
- ¼ teaspoon garlic powder
- Pinch of red pepper flakes

Preparation Instructions :

1. Place the beef in a gallon-size resealable bag. In a small bowl, whisk together the olive oil, balsamic vinegar, Worcestershire sauce, and garlic. Pour the marinade over

the beef, massaging gently to coat, and seal the bag. Let sit at room temperature for an hour or refrigerate overnight.

2. To make the herb butter: In a small bowl, mix the butter with the parsley, salt, rosemary, garlic powder, and red pepper flakes until smooth. Cover and refrigerate until ready to use.

3. Preheat the air fryer to 204ºC.

4. Remove the beef from the marinade (discard the marinade) and place the beef in the air fryer basket. Pausing halfway through the cooking time to turn the meat, air fry for 20 to 25 minutes, until a thermometer inserted into the thickest part indicates the desired doneness, 52ºC (rare) to 64ºC (medium). Let the beef rest for 10 minutes before slicing. Serve topped with the herb butter.

Beef and Spinach Rolls

Prep time: 10 minutes
Cook time: 14 minutes
Serves 2

Ingredients :

- 3 teaspoons pesto
- 900 g beef bavette or skirt steak
- 6 slices low-moisture Mozarella or other melting cheese
- 85 g roasted red peppers
- 180 ml baby spinach
- 1 teaspoon sea salt
- 1 teaspoon black pepper

Preparation Instructions :

1. Preheat the air fryer to 204ºC.

2. Spoon equal amounts of the pesto onto each steak and spread it across evenly.

3. Put the cheese, roasted red peppers and spinach on top of the meat, about three-quarters of the way down.

4. Roll the steak up, holding it in place with toothpicks. Sprinkle with the sea salt and pepper.

5. Put inside the air fryer and air fry for 14 minutes, turning halfway through the cooking time.

6. Allow the beef to rest for 10 minutes before slicing up and serving.

Cheddar Bacon Burst with Spinach

Prep time: 5 minutes
Cook time: 60 minutes
Serves 8

Ingredients :

- 30 slices bacon
- 1 tablespoon Chipotle chilli powder
- 2 teaspoons Italian seasoning
- 120 ml Cheddar cheese
- 1 L raw spinach

Preparation Instructions :

1. Preheat the air fryer to 192ºC.

2. Weave the bacon into 15 vertical pieces and 12 horizontal pieces. Cut the extra 3 in half to fill in the rest, horizontally.

3. Season the bacon with Chipotle chilli powder and Italian seasoning.

4. Add the cheese to the bacon.

5. Add the spinach and press down to compress.

6. Tightly roll up the woven bacon.

7. Line a baking sheet with kitchen foil and add plenty of salt to it.

8. Put the bacon on top of a cooling rack and put that on top of the baking sheet.

9. Bake for 60 minutes.

10. Let cool for 15 minutes before slicing and serving.

Pigs in a Blanket

Prep time: 10 minutes

Cook time: 7 minutes

Serves 2

Ingredients :

- 120 ml shredded Mozzarella cheese
- 2 tablespoons blanched finely ground almond flour
- 30 g full-fat cream cheese
- 2 (110 g) beef smoked sausage, cut in two
- ½ teaspoon sesame seeds

Preparation Instructions :

1. Place Mozzarella, almond flour, and cream cheese in a large microwave-safe bowl. Microwave for 45 seconds and stir until smooth. Roll dough into a ball and cut in half.
2. Press each half out into a 4 × 5-inch rectangle. Roll one sausage up in each dough half and press seams closed. Sprinkle the top with sesame seeds.
3. Place each wrapped sausage into the air fryer basket.
4. Adjust the temperature to 204°C and air fry for 7 minutes.
5. The outside will be golden when completely cooked. Serve immediately.

Savory Sausage Cobbler

Prep time: 15 minutes

Cook time: 34 minutes

Serves 4

Ingredients :

Filling:

- 450 g Italian-seasoned sausage meat, removed from casing
- 235 ml sliced mushrooms
- 1 teaspoon fine sea salt
- 475 ml marinara sauce

Biscuits:

- 3 large egg whites
- 180 ml blanched almond flour
- 1 teaspoon baking powder
- ¼ teaspoon fine sea salt
- 2½ tablespoons very cold unsalted butter, cut into ¼-inch pieces
- Fresh basil leaves, for garnish

Preparation Instructions :

1. Preheat the air fryer to 204°C.
2. Place the sausage in a pie pan (or a pan that fits into your air fryer). Use your hands to break up the sausage and spread it evenly on the bottom of the pan. Place the pan in the air fryer and air fry for 5 minutes.
3. Remove the pan from the air fryer and use a fork or metal spatula to crumble the sausage more. Season the mushrooms with the salt and add them to the pie pan. Stir to combine the mushrooms and sausage, then return the pan to the air fryer and air fry for 4 minutes, or until the mushrooms are soft and the sausage is cooked through.
4. Remove the pan from the air fryer. Add the marinara sauce and stir well. Set aside.
5. Make the biscuits: Place the egg whites in a large mixing bowl or the bowl of a stand mixer. Using a hand mixer or stand mixer, whip the egg whites until stiff peaks form.
6. In a medium-sized bowl, whisk together the almond flour, baking powder, and salt, then cut in the butter. Gently fold the flour mixture into the egg whites with a rubber spatula.
7. Using a large spoon or ice cream scoop, spoon one-quarter of the dough on top of the sausage mixture, making sure the butter stays in separate clumps. Repeat

with the remaining dough, spacing the biscuits about 1 inch apart.

8. Place the pan in the air fryer and cook for 5 minutes, then lower the heat to 164°C and bake for another 15 to 20 minutes, until the biscuits are golden brown. Serve garnished with fresh basil leaves.

9. Store leftovers in an airtight container in the refrigerator for up to 3 days. Reheat in a preheated 176°C air fryer for 5 minutes, or until warmed through.

Sausage and Courgette Lasagna

Prep time: 25 minutes
Cook time: 56 minutes
Serves 4

Ingredients :

- 1 courgette
- Avocado oil spray
- 170 g hot Italian-seasoned sausage, casings removed
- 60 g mushrooms, stemmed and sliced
- 1 teaspoon minced garlic
- 235 ml keto-friendly marinara sauce
- 180 ml ricotta cheese
- 235 ml shredded gruyere cheese, divided
- 120 ml finely grated Parmesan cheese
- Sea salt and freshly ground black pepper, to taste
- Fresh basil, for garnish

Preparation Instructions :

1. Cut the courgette into long thin slices using a mandoline slicer or sharp knife. Spray both sides of the slices with oil.

2. Place the slices in a single layer in the air fryer basket, working in batches if necessary. Set the air fryer to 164°C and air fry for 4 to 6 minutes, until most of the moisture has been released from the courgette.

3. Place a large skillet over medium-high heat. Crumble the sausage into the hot skillet and cook for 6 minutes, breaking apart the meat with the back of a spoon. Remove the sausage from the skillet, leaving any fats that remain. Add the mushrooms to the skillet and cook for 10 minutes, until the liquid nearly evaporates. Add the garlic and cook for 1 minute more. Stir in the marinara and cook for 2 more minutes.

4. In a medium bowl, combine the ricotta cheese, 120 ml of gruyere cheese, Parmesan cheese, and salt and pepper to taste.

5. Spread 60 ml of the meat sauce in the bottom of a deep pan (or other pan that fits inside your air fryer). Top with half of the courgette slices. Add half of the cheese mixture. Top the cheese with half of the remaining meat sauce. Layer the remaining courgette over the meat sauce and top with the remaining cheese mixture. Top the lasagna with the remaining 120 ml of fontina cheese.

6. Cover the lasagna with aluminum foil or parchment paper and place it in the air fryer. Bake for 25 minutes. Remove the foil and cook for 8 to 10 minutes more.

7. Allow the lasagna to rest for 15 minutes before cutting and serving. Garnish with basil.

Greek Pork with Tzatziki Sauce

Prep time: 30 minutes
Cook time: 50 minutes
Serves 4

Ingredients :

- Greek Pork:
- 900 g pork loin roasting joint
- Salt and black pepper, to taste
- 1 teaspoon smoked paprika
- ½ teaspoon mustard seeds
- ½ teaspoon celery salt
- 1 teaspoon fennel seeds
- 1 teaspoon chili powder
- 1 teaspoon turmeric powder
- ½ teaspoon ground ginger
- 2 tablespoons olive oil
- 2 cloves garlic, finely chopped
- Tzatziki:
- ½ cucumber, finely chopped and squeezed
- 235 ml full-fat Greek yogurt
- 1 garlic clove, minced
- 1 tablespoon extra-virgin olive oil
- 1 teaspoon balsamic vinegar
- 1 teaspoon minced fresh dill
- A pinch of salt

Preparation Instructions :

1. Toss all ingredients for Greek pork in a large mixing bowl. Toss until the meat is well coated.
2. Cook in the preheated air fryer at 182°C for 30 minutes; turn over and cook another 20 minutes.
3. Meanwhile, prepare the tzatziki by mixing all the tzatziki ingredients. Place in your refrigerator until ready to use.
4. Serve the pork sirloin roast with the chilled tzatziki on the side. Enjoy!

Kheema Meatloaf

Prep time: 10 minutes
Cook time: 15 minutes
Serves 4

Ingredients :

- 450 g 85% lean beef mince
- 2 large eggs, lightly beaten
- 235 ml diced brown onion
- 60 ml chopped fresh coriander
- 1 tablespoon minced fresh ginger
- 1 tablespoon minced garlic
- 2 teaspoons garam masala
- 1 teaspoon coarse or flaky salt
- 1 teaspoon ground turmeric
- 1 teaspoon cayenne pepper
- ½ teaspoon ground cinnamon
- ⅛ teaspoon ground cardamom

Preparation Instructions :

1. In a large bowl, gently mix the beef mince, eggs, onion, coriander, ginger, garlic, garam masala, salt, turmeric, cayenne, cinnamon, and cardamom until thoroughly combined.
2. Place the seasoned meat in a baking pan. Place the pan in the air fryer basket. Set the air fryer to 176°C for 15 minutes. Use a meat thermometer to ensure the meat loaf has reached an internal temperature of 72°C (medium).
3. Drain the fat and liquid from the pan and let stand for 5 minutes before slicing.
4. Slice and serve hot.

Greek Stuffed Fillet

Prep time: 10 minutes
Cook time: 10 minutes
Serves 4

Ingredients :

- 680 g venison or beef fillet, pounded to ¼ inch thick
- 3 teaspoons fine sea salt
- 1 teaspoon ground black pepper
- 60 g creamy goat cheese
- 120 ml crumbled feta cheese (about 60 g)
- 60 ml finely chopped onions
- 2 cloves garlic, minced
- For Garnish/Serving (Optional):
- Yellow/American mustard
- Halved cherry tomatoes
- Extra-virgin olive oil
- Sprigs of fresh rosemary
- Lavender flowers

Preparation Instructions :

1. Spray the air fryer basket with avocado oil. Preheat the air fryer to 204°C.
2. Season the fillet on all sides with the salt and pepper.
3. In a medium-sized mixing bowl, combine the goat cheese, feta, onions, and garlic. Place the mixture in the center of the tenderloin. Starting at the end closest to you, tightly roll the tenderloin like a jelly roll. Tie the rolled tenderloin tightly with kitchen twine.
4. Place the meat in the air fryer basket and air fry for 5 minutes. Flip the meat over and cook for another 5 minutes, or until the internal temperature reaches 57°C for medium-rare.
5. To serve, smear a line of yellow mustard on a platter, then place the meat next to it and add halved cherry tomatoes on the side, if desired. Drizzle with olive oil and garnish with rosemary sprigs and lavender flowers, if desired.
6. Best served fresh. Store leftovers in an airtight container in the fridge for 3 days. Reheat in a preheated 176°C air fryer for 4 minutes, or until heated through.

Air Fryer Chicken-Fried Steak

Prep time: 5 minutes
Cook time: 20 minutes
Serves 4

Ingredients :

- 450 g beef braising steak
- 700 ml low-fat milk, divided
- 1 teaspoon dried thyme
- 1 teaspoon dried rosemary
- 2 medium egg whites
- 235 ml gluten-free breadcrumbs
- 120 ml coconut flour
- 1 tablespoon Cajun seasoning

Preparation Instructions :

1. In a bowl, marinate the steak in 475 ml of milk for 30 to 45 minutes.
2. Remove the steak from milk, shake off the excess liquid, and season with the thyme and rosemary. Discard the milk.
3. In a shallow bowl, beat the egg whites with the remaining 235 ml of milk.
4. In a separate shallow bowl, combine the breadcrumbs, coconut flour, and seasoning.
5. Dip the steak in the egg white mixture then dredge in the breadcrumb mixture, coating well.
6. Place the steak in the basket of an air fryer.
7. Set the air fryer to 200°C, close, and cook for 10 minutes.
8. Open the air fryer, turn the steaks, close, and cook for 10 minutes. Let rest for 5 minutes.

Bacon-Wrapped Hot Dogs with Mayo-Ketchup Sauce

Prep time: 5 minutes
Cook time: 10 to 12 minutes
Serves 5

Ingredients :

- 10 thin slices of bacon
- 5 pork hot dogs, halved
- 1 teaspoon cayenne pepper
- Sauce:
- 60 ml mayonnaise
- 4 tablespoons ketchup
- 1 teaspoon rice vinegar
- 1 teaspoon chili powder

Preparation Instructions :

1. Preheat the air fryer to 200°C.
2. Arrange the slices of bacon on a clean work surface. One by one, place the halved hot dog on one end of each slice, season with cayenne pepper and wrap the hot dog with the bacon slices and secure with toothpicks as needed.
3. Work in batches, place half the wrapped hot dogs in the air fryer basket and air fry for 10 to 12 minutes or until the bacon becomes browned and crispy.
4. Make the sauce: Stir all the ingredients for the sauce in a small bowl. Wrap the bowl in plastic and set in the refrigerator until ready to serve.
5. Transfer the hot dogs to a platter and serve hot with the sauce.

Stuffed Beef Fillet with Feta Cheese

Prep time: 10 minutes
Cook time: 10 minutes
Serves 4

Ingredients :

- 680 g beef fillet, pounded to ¼ inch thick
- 3 teaspoons sea salt
- 1 teaspoon ground black pepper
- 60 g creamy goat cheese
- 120 ml crumbled feta cheese
- 60 ml finely chopped onions
- 2 cloves garlic, minced
- Cooking spray

Preparation Instructions :

1. Preheat the air fryer to 204°C. Spritz the air fryer basket with cooking spray.
2. Unfold the beef on a clean work surface. Rub the salt and pepper all over the beef to season.
3. Make the filling for the stuffed beef fillet: Combine the goat cheese, feta, onions, and garlic in a medium bowl. Stir until well blended.
4. Spoon the mixture in the center of the fillet. Roll the fillet up tightly like rolling a burrito and use some kitchen twine to tie the fillet.
5. Arrange the fillet in the air fryer basket and air fry for 10 minutes, flipping the fillet halfway through to ensure even cooking, or until an instant-read thermometer inserted in the center of the fillet registers 57°C for medium-rare.
6. Transfer to a platter and serve immediately.

Deconstructed Chicago Dogs

Prep time: 10 minutes

Cook time: 7 minutes

Serves 4

Ingredients :

- 4 hot dogs
- 2 large dill pickles
- 60 ml diced onions
- 1 tomato, cut into ½-inch dice
- 4 pickled or brined jalapeno peppers, diced
- For Garnish (Optional):
- Wholegrain or Dijon mustard
- Celery salt
- Poppy seeds

Preparation Instructions :

1. Spray the air fryer basket with avocado oil. Preheat the air fryer to 204°C.
2. Place the hot dogs in the air fryer basket and air fry for 5 to 7 minutes, until hot and slightly crispy.
3. While the hot dogs cook, quarter one of the dill pickles lengthwise, so that you have 4 pickle spears. Finely dice the other pickle.
4. When the hot dogs are done, transfer them to a serving platter and arrange them in a row, alternating with the pickle spears. Top with the diced pickles, onions, tomato, and jalapeno peppers. Drizzle mustard on top and garnish with celery salt and poppy seeds, if desired.
5. Best served fresh. Store leftover hot dogs in an airtight container in the refrigerator for up to 3 days. Reheat in a preheated 200°C air fryer for 2 minutes, or until warmed through.

Fillet with Crispy Shallots

Prep time: 30 minutes

Cook time: 18 to 20 minutes

Serves 6

Ingredients :

- 680 g beef fillet steaks
- Sea salt and freshly ground black pepper, to taste
- 4 medium shallots
- 1 teaspoon olive oil or avocado oil

Preparation Instructions :

1. Season both sides of the steaks with salt and pepper, and let them sit at room temperature for 45 minutes.
2. Set the air fryer to 204°C and let it preheat for 5 minutes.
3. Working in batches if necessary, place the steaks in the air fryer basket in a single layer and air fry for 5 minutes. Flip and cook for 5 minutes longer, until an instant-read thermometer inserted in the center of the steaks registers 49°C for medium-rare (or as desired). Remove the steaks and tent with aluminum foil to rest.
4. Set the air fryer to 149°C. In a medium bowl, toss the shallots with the oil. Place the shallots in the basket and air fry for 5 minutes, then give them a toss and cook for 3 to 5 minutes more, until crispy and golden brown.
5. Place the steaks on serving plates and arrange the shallots on top.

Lemon Pepper Prawns

Prep time: 15 minutes
Cook time: 8 minutes
Serves 2

Ingredients :

- Olive or vegetable oil, for spraying
- 340 g medium raw prawns, peeled and deveined
- 3 tablespoons lemon juice
- 1 tablespoon olive oil
- 1 teaspoon lemon pepper
- ¼ teaspoon paprika
- ¼ teaspoon granulated garlic

Preparation Instructions :

1. Preheat the air fryer to 204°C. Line the air fryer basket with baking paper and spray lightly with oil.
2. In a medium bowl, toss together the prawns, lemon juice, olive oil, lemon pepper, paprika, and garlic until evenly coated.
3. Place the prawns in the prepared basket.
4. Cook for 6 to 8 minutes, or until pink and firm. Serve immediately.

Tuna-Stuffed Quinoa Patties

Prep time: 10 minutes
Cook time: 15 minutes
Serves 4

Ingredients :

- 35 g quinoa
- 4 slices white bread with crusts removed
- 120 ml milk
- 3 eggs
- 280 g tuna packed in olive oil, drained
- 2 to 3 lemons
- Kosher or coarse sea salt, and pepper, to taste
- 150 g panko bread crumbs
- Vegetable oil, for spraying
- Lemon wedges, for serving

Preparation Instructions :

1. Rinse the quinoa in a fine-mesh sieve until the water runs clear. Bring 1 liter of salted water to a boil. Add the quinoa, cover, and reduce heat to low. Simmer the quinoa covered until most of the water is absorbed and the quinoa is tender, 15 to 20 minutes. Drain and allow to cool to room temperature. Meanwhile, soak the bread in the milk.
2. Mix the drained quinoa with the soaked bread and 2 of the eggs in a large bowl and mix thoroughly. In a medium bowl, combine the tuna, the remaining egg, and the juice and zest of 1 of the lemons. Season well with salt and pepper. Spread the panko on a plate.
3. Scoop up approximately 60 g of the quinoa mixture and flatten into a patty. Place a heaping tablespoon of the tuna mixture in the center of the patty and close the quinoa around the tuna. Flatten the patty slightly to create an oval-shaped croquette. Dredge both sides of the croquette in the panko. Repeat with the remaining quinoa and tuna.
4. Spray the air fryer basket with oil to prevent sticking, and preheat the air fryer to 204°C. Arrange 4 or 5 of the croquettes in the basket, taking care to avoid overcrowding. Spray the tops of the croquettes with oil. Air fry for 8

minutes until the top side is browned and crispy. Carefully turn the croquettes over and spray the second side with oil. Air fry until the second side is browned and crispy, another 7 minutes. Repeat with the remaining croquettes.

5. Serve the croquetas warm with plenty of lemon wedges for spritzing.

Southern-Style Catfish

Prep time: 10 minutes
Cook time: 12 minutes
Serves 4

Ingredients :

- 4 (200 g) catfish fillets
- 80 ml heavy whipping cream
- 1 tablespoon lemon juice
- 110 g blanched finely ground almond flour
- 2 teaspoons Old Bay seasoning
- ½ teaspoon salt
- ¼ teaspoon ground black pepper

Preparation Instructions :

1. Place catfish fillets into a large bowl with cream and pour in lemon juice. Stir to coat.
2. In a separate large bowl, mix flour and Old Bay seasoning.
3. Remove each fillet and gently shake off excess cream. Sprinkle with salt and pepper. Press each fillet gently into flour mixture on both sides to coat.
4. Place fillets into ungreased air fryer basket. Adjust the temperature to 204°C and air fry for 12 minutes, turning fillets halfway through cooking. Catfish will be golden brown and have an internal temperature of at least 64°C when done. Serve warm.

Scallops and Spinach with Cream Sauce

Prep time: 5 minutes
Cook time: 10 minutes
Serves 2

Ingredients :

- Vegetable oil spray
- 280 g frozen spinach, thawed and drained
- 8 jumbo sea scallops
- Kosher or coarse sea salt, and black pepper, to taste
- 180 ml heavy cream
- 1 tablespoon tomato paste
- 1 tablespoon chopped fresh basil
- 1 teaspoon minced garlic

Preparation Instructions :

1. Spray a baking pan with vegetable oil spray. Spread the thawed spinach in an even layer in the bottom of the pan.
2. Spray both sides of the scallops with vegetable oil spray. Season lightly with salt and pepper. Arrange the scallops on top of the spinach.
3. In a small bowl, whisk together the cream, tomato paste, basil, garlic, ½ teaspoon salt, and ½ teaspoon pepper. Pour the sauce over the scallops and spinach.
4. Place the pan in the air fryer basket. Set the air fryer to 176°C for 10 minutes. Use a meat thermometer to ensure the scallops have an internal temperature of 56°C.

Jalea

Prep time: 20 minutes
Cook time: 10 minutes
Serves 4

Ingredients :

Salsa Criolla:

- ½ red onion, thinly sliced
- 2 tomatoes, diced
- 1 serrano or jalapeño pepper, deseeded and diced
- 1 clove garlic, minced
- 5 g chopped fresh coriander
- Pinch of kosher or coarse sea salt
- 3 limes

Fried Seafood:

- 455 g firm, white-fleshed fish such as cod (add an extra 230 g fish if not using prawns)
- 20 large or jumbo prawns, peeled and deveined
- 30 g plain flour
- 40 g cornflour
- 1 teaspoon garlic powder
- 1 teaspoon kosher or coarse sea salt
- ¼ teaspoon cayenne pepper
- 240 g panko bread crumbs
- 2 eggs, beaten with 2 tablespoons water
- Vegetable oil, for spraying
- Mayonnaise or tartar sauce, for serving (optional)

Preparation Instructions :

1. To make the Salsa Criolla, combine the red onion, tomatoes, pepper, garlic, cilantro, and salt in a medium bowl. Add the juice and zest of 2 of the limes. Refrigerate the salad while you make the fish.

2. To make the seafood, cut the fish fillets into strips approximately 2 inches long and 1 inch wide. Place the flour, cornstarch, garlic powder, salt, and cayenne pepper on a plate and whisk to combine. Place the panko on a separate plate. Dredge the fish strips in the seasoned flour mixture, shaking off any excess. Dip the strips in the egg mixture, coating them completely, then dredge in the panko, shaking off any excess. Place the fish strips on a plate or rack. Repeat with the prawns, if using.

3. Spray the air fryer basket with oil, and preheat the air fryer to 204ºC. Working in 2 or 3 batches, arrange the fish and prawns in a single layer in the basket, taking care not to crowd the basket. Spray with oil. Air fry for 5 minutes, then flip and air fry for another 4 to 5 minutes until the outside is brown and crisp and the inside of the fish is opaque and flakes easily with a fork. Repeat with the remaining seafood.

4. Place the fried seafood on a platter. Use a slotted spoon to remove the salsa criolla from the bowl, leaving behind any liquid that has accumulated. Place the salsa criolla on top of the fried seafood. Serve immediately with the remaining lime, cut into wedges, and mayonnaise or tartar sauce as desired.

Paprika Prawns

Prep time: 5 minutes
Cook time: 6 minutes
Serves 2

Ingredients :

- 230 g medium prawns, peeled and deveined
- 2 tablespoons salted butter, melted
- 1 teaspoon paprika
- ½ teaspoon garlic powder
- ¼ teaspoon onion powder
- ½ teaspoon Old Bay seasoning

Preparation Instructions :

1. Toss all ingredients together in a large bowl. Place prawns into the air fryer basket.
2. Adjust the temperature to 204ºC and set the timer for 6 minutes.
3. Turn the prawns halfway through the cooking time to ensure even cooking. Serve immediately.

Coconut Cream Mackerel

Prep time: 10 minutes
Cook time: 6 minutes
Serves 4

Ingredients :

- 900 g mackerel fillet
- 240 ml coconut cream
- 1 teaspoon ground coriander
- 1 teaspoon cumin seeds
- 1 garlic clove, peeled, chopped

Preparation Instructions :

1. Chop the mackerel roughly and sprinkle it with coconut cream, ground coriander, cumin seeds, and garlic.
2. Then put the fish in the air fryer and cook at 204ºC for 6 minutes.

Panko Crab Sticks with Mayo Sauce

Prep time: 5 minutes
Cook time: 12 minutes
Serves 4

Ingredients :

- Crab Sticks:
- 2 eggs
- 120 g plain flour
- 50 g panko bread crumbs
- 1 tablespoon Old Bay seasoning
- 455 g crab sticks
- Cooking spray
- Mayo Sauce:
- 115 g mayonnaise
- 1 lime, juiced
- 2 garlic cloves, minced

Preparation Instructions :

1. Preheat air fryer to 200ºC.
2. In a bowl, beat the eggs. In a shallow bowl, place the flour. In another shallow bowl, thoroughly combine the panko bread crumbs and old bay seasoning.
3. Dredge the crab sticks in the flour, shaking off any excess, then in the beaten eggs, finally press them in the bread crumb mixture to coat well.
4. Arrange the crab sticks in the air fryer basket and spray with cooking spray.
5. Air fry for 12 minutes until golden brown. Flip the crab sticks halfway through the cooking time.
6. Meanwhile, make the sauce by whisking together the mayo, lime juice, and garlic in a small bowl.
7. Serve the crab sticks with the mayo sauce on the side.

Seasoned Breaded Prawns

Prep time: 15 minutes

Cook time: 10 to 15 minutes

Serves 4

Ingredients :

- 2 teaspoons Old Bay seasoning, divided
- ½ teaspoon garlic powder
- ½ teaspoon onion powder
- 455 g large prawns, peeled and deveined, with tails on
- 2 large eggs
- 75 g whole-wheat panko bread crumbs
- Cooking spray

Preparation Instructions :

1. Preheat the air fryer to 192ºC.
2. Spray the air fryer basket lightly with cooking spray.
3. In a medium bowl, mix together 1 teaspoon of Old Bay seasoning, garlic powder, and onion powder. Add the prawns and toss with the seasoning mix to lightly coat.
4. In a separate small bowl, whisk the eggs with 1 teaspoon water.
5. In a shallow bowl, mix together the remaining 1 teaspoon Old Bay seasoning and the panko bread crumbs.
6. Dip each prawns in the egg mixture and dredge in the bread crumb mixture to evenly coat.
7. Place the prawns in the air fryer basket, in a single layer. Lightly spray the prawns with cooking spray. You many need to cook the prawns in batches.
8. Air fry for 10 to 15 minutes, or until the prawns is cooked through and crispy, shaking the basket at 5-minute intervals to redistribute and evenly cook.
9. Serve immediately.

Paprika Crab Burgers

Prep time: 30 minutes

Cook time: 14 minutes

Serves 3

Ingredients :

- 2 eggs, beaten
- 1 shallot, chopped
- 2 garlic cloves, crushed
- 1 tablespoon olive oil
- 1 teaspoon yellow mustard
- 1 teaspoon fresh coriander, chopped
- 280 g crab meat
- 1 teaspoon smoked paprika
- ½ teaspoon ground black pepper
- Sea salt, to taste
- 70 g Parmesan cheese

Preparation Instructions :

1. In a mixing bowl, thoroughly combine the eggs, shallot, garlic, olive oil, mustard, coriander, crab meat, paprika, black pepper, and salt. Mix until well combined.
2. Shape the mixture into 6 patties. Roll the crab patties over grated Parmesan cheese, coating well on all sides. Place in your refrigerator for 2 hours.
3. Spritz the crab patties with cooking oil on both sides. Cook in the preheated air fryer at 182ºC for 14 minutes. Serve on dinner rolls if desired. Bon appétit!

Fish Croquettes with Lemon-Dill Aioli

Prep time: 15 minutes
Cook time: 10 minutes
Serves 4

Ingredients :

Croquettes:
- 3 large eggs, divided
- 340 g raw cod fillet, flaked apart with two forks
- 60 ml skimmed milk
- 190 g boxed instant mashed potatoes
- 2 teaspoons olive oil
- 8 g chopped fresh dill
- 1 shallot, minced
- 1 large garlic clove, minced
- 120 g breadcrumbs plus 2 tablespoons, divided
- 1 teaspoon fresh lemon juice
- 1 teaspoon kosher or coarse sea salt
- ½ teaspoon dried thyme
- ¼ teaspoon freshly ground black pepper
- Cooking spray
- Lemon-Dill Aioli:
- 5 tablespoons mayonnaise
- Juice of ½ lemon
- 1 tablespoon chopped fresh dill

Preparation Instructions :

1. For the croquettes: In a medium bowl, lightly beat 2 of the eggs. Add the fish, milk, instant mashed potatoes, olive oil, dill, shallot, and garlic, 2 tablespoons of the bread crumbs, lemon juice, salt, thyme, and pepper. Mix to thoroughly combine. Place in the refrigerator for 30 minutes.

2. For the lemon-dill aioli: In a small bowl, combine the mayonnaise, lemon juice, and dill. Set aside.

3. Measure out about 3½ tablespoons of the fish mixture and gently roll in your hands to form a log about 3 inches long. Repeat to make a total of 12 logs.

4. Beat the remaining egg in a small bowl. Place the remaining ¾ cup bread crumbs in a separate bowl. Dip the croquettes in the egg, then coat in the bread crumbs, gently pressing to adhere. Place on a work surface and spray both sides with cooking spray.

5. Preheat the air fryer to 176ºC.

6. Working in batches, arrange a single layer of the croquettes in the air fryer basket. Air fry for about 10 minutes, flipping halfway, until golden.

7. Serve with the aioli for dipping.

Sea Bass with Roasted Root Vegetables

Prep time: 10 minutes
Cook time: 15 minutes
Serves 4

Ingredients :
- 1 carrot, diced small
- 1 parsnip, diced small
- 1 swede, diced small
- 60 ml olive oil
- 1 teaspoon salt, divided
- 4 sea bass fillets
- ½ teaspoon onion powder
- 2 garlic cloves, minced
- 1 lemon, sliced, plus additional wedges for serving

Preparation Instructions :

1. Preheat the air fryer to 192ºC.

2. In a small bowl, toss the carrot, parsnip, and swede with olive oil and 1 teaspoon salt.

3. Lightly season the sea bass with the remaining 1 teaspoon of salt and the

onion powder, then place it into the air fryer basket in a single layer.

4. Spread the garlic over the top of each fillet, then cover with lemon slices.

5. Pour the prepared vegetables into the basket around and on top of the fish. Roast for 15 minutes.

6. Serve with additional lemon wedges if desired.

Tuna with Herbs

Prep time: 20 minutes
Cook time: 17 minutes
Serves 4

Ingredients :

- 1 tablespoon butter, melted
- 1 medium-sized leek, thinly sliced
- 1 tablespoon chicken stock
- 1 tablespoon dry white wine
- 455 g tuna
- ½ teaspoon red pepper flakes, crushed
- Sea salt and ground black pepper, to taste
- ½ teaspoon dried rosemary
- ½ teaspoon dried basil
- ½ teaspoon dried thyme
- 2 small ripe tomatoes, puréed
- 120 g Parmesan cheese, grated

Preparation Instructions :

1. Melt ½ tablespoon of butter in a sauté pan over medium-high heat. Now, cook the leek and garlic until tender and aromatic. Add the stock and wine to deglaze the pan.

2. Preheat the air fryer to 188°C.

3. Grease a casserole dish with the remaining ½ tablespoon of melted butter. Place the fish in the casserole dish. Add the seasonings. Top with the sautéed leek mixture. Add the tomato purée. Cook for 10 minutes in the preheated air fryer. Top

with grated Parmesan cheese; cook an additional 7 minutes until the crumbs are golden. Bon appétit!

Chilean Sea Bass with Olive Relish

Prep time: 10 minutes
Cook time: 10 minutes
Serves 2

Ingredients :

- Olive oil spray
- 2 (170 g) Chilean sea bass fillets or other firm-fleshed white fish
- 3 tablespoons extra-virgin olive oil
- ½ teaspoon ground cumin
- ½ teaspoon kosher or coarse sea salt
- ½ teaspoon black pepper
- 60 g pitted green olives, diced
- 10 g finely diced onion
- 1 teaspoon chopped capers

Preparation Instructions :

1. Spray the air fryer basket with the olive oil spray. Drizzle the fillets with the olive oil and sprinkle with the cumin, salt, and pepper. Place the fish in the air fryer basket. Set the air fryer to 164°C for 10 minutes, or until the fish flakes easily with a fork.

2. Meanwhile, in a small bowl, stir together the olives, onion, and capers.

3. Serve the fish topped with the relish.

Lemon-Tarragon Fish en Papillote

Prep time: 10 minutes

Cook time: 15 minutes

Serves 2

Ingredients :

- 2 tablespoons salted butter, melted
- 1 tablespoon fresh lemon juice
- ½ teaspoon dried tarragon, crushed, or 2 sprigs fresh tarragon
- 1 teaspoon kosher or coarse sea salt
- 85 g julienned carrots
- 435 g julienned fennel, or 1 stalk julienned celery
- 75 g thinly sliced red bell pepper
- 2 cod fillets, 170 g each, thawed if frozen
- Vegetable oil spray
- ½ teaspoon black pepper

Preparation Instructions :

1. In a medium bowl, combine the butter, lemon juice, tarragon, and ½ teaspoon of the salt. Whisk well until you get a creamy sauce. Add the carrots, fennel, and bell pepper and toss to combine; set aside.
2. Cut two squares of baking paper each large enough to hold one fillet and half the vegetables. Spray the fillets with vegetable oil spray. Season both sides with the remaining ½ teaspoon salt and the black pepper.
3. Lay one fillet down on each baking paper square. Top each with half the vegetables. Pour any remaining sauce over the vegetables.
4. Fold over the baking paper and crimp the sides in small, tight folds to hold the fish, vegetables, and sauce securely inside the packet. Place the packets in the air fryer basket. Set the air fryer to 176°C for 15 minutes.
5. Transfer each packet to a plate. Cut open with scissors just before serving (be careful, as the steam inside will be hot).

Garlic Soy Chicken Thighs

Prep time: 10 minutes
Cook time: 30 minutes
Serves 1 to 2

Ingredients :

- 2 tablespoons chicken stock
- 2 tablespoons reduced-sodium soy sauce
- 1½ tablespoons sugar
- 4 garlic cloves, smashed and peeled
- 2 large spring onions, cut into 2- to 3-inch batons, plus more, thinly sliced, for garnish
- 2 bone-in, skin-on chicken thighs (198 to 225 g each)

Preparation Instructions :

1. Preheat the air fryer to 190°C.
2. In a metal cake pan, combine the chicken stock, soy sauce, and sugar and stir until the sugar dissolves. Add the garlic cloves, spring onions, and chicken thighs, turning the thighs to coat them in the marinade, then resting them skin-side up. Place the pan in the air fryer and bake, flipping the thighs every 5 minutes after the first 10 minutes, until the chicken is cooked through and the marinade is reduced to a sticky glaze over the chicken, about 30 minutes.
3. Remove the pan from the air fryer and serve the chicken thighs warm, with any remaining glaze spooned over top and sprinkled with more sliced spring onions.

Chicken Burgers with Ham and Cheese

Prep time: 12 minutes
Cook time: 13 to 16 minutes
Serves 4

Ingredients :

- 40 g soft bread crumbs
- 3 tablespoons milk
- 1 egg, beaten
- ½ teaspoon dried thyme
- Pinch salt
- Freshly ground black pepper, to taste
- 570 g chicken mince
- 70 g finely chopped ham
- 75 g grated Gouda cheese
- Olive oil for misting

Preparation Instructions :

1. Preheat the air fryer to 180°C.
2. In a medium bowl, combine the bread crumbs, milk, egg, thyme, salt, and pepper. Add the chicken and mix gently but thoroughly with clean hands.
3. Form the chicken into eight thin patties and place on waxed paper.
4. Top four of the patties with the ham and cheese. Top with remaining four patties and gently press the edges together to seal, so the ham and cheese mixture is in the middle of the burger.
5. Place the burgers in the basket and mist with olive oil. Bake for 13 to 16 minutes or until the chicken is thoroughly cooked to 76°C as measured with a meat thermometer. Serve immediately.

Coconut Chicken Meatballs

Prep time: 10 minutes
Cook time: 14 minutes
Serves 4

Ingredients :

- 450 g chicken mince
- 2 spring onions, finely chopped
- 20 g chopped fresh corinader leaves
- 20 g unsweetened shredded coconut
- 1 tablespoon hoisin sauce
- 1 tablespoon soy sauce
- 2 teaspoons Sriracha or other hot sauce
- 1 teaspoon toasted sesame oil
- ½ teaspoon kosher salt
- 1 teaspoon black pepper

Preparation Instructions :

1. In a large bowl, gently mix the chicken, spring onions, coriander, coconut, hoisin, soy sauce, Sriracha, sesame oil, salt, and pepper until thoroughly combined (the mixture will be wet and sticky).
2. Place a sheet of parchment paper in the air fryer basket. Using a small scoop or teaspoon, drop rounds of the mixture in a single layer onto the parchment paper.
3. Set the air fryer to 180°C for 10 minutes, turning the meatballs halfway through the cooking time. Raise the air fryer temperature to 200°C and cook for 4 minutes more to brown the outsides of the meatballs. Use a meat thermometer to ensure the meatballs have reached an internal temperature of 76°C.
4. Transfer the meatballs to a serving platter. Repeat with any remaining chicken mixture.

Lemon Chicken with Garlic

Prep time: 5 minutes
Cook time: 20 to 25 minutes
Serves 4

Ingredients :

- 8 bone-in chicken thighs, skin on
- 1 tablespoon olive oil
- 1½ teaspoons lemon-pepper seasoning
- ½ teaspoon paprika
- ½ teaspoon garlic powder
- ¼ teaspoon freshly ground black pepper
- Juice of ½ lemon

Preparation Instructions :

1. Preheat the air fryer to 180°C.
2. Place the chicken in a large bowl and drizzle with the olive oil. Top with the lemon-pepper seasoning, paprika, garlic powder, and freshly ground black pepper. Toss until thoroughly coated.
3. Working in batches if necessary, arrange the chicken in a single layer in the basket of the air fryer. Pausing halfway through the cooking time to turn the chicken, air fry for 20 to 25 minutes, until a thermometer inserted into the thickest piece registers 76°C.
4. Transfer the chicken to a serving platter and squeeze the lemon juice over the top.

Chicken Hand Pies

Prep time: 30 minutes
Cook time: 10 minutes per batch
Makes 8 pies

Ingredients :

- 180 ml chicken broth
- 130 g frozen mixed peas and carrots
- 140 g cooked chicken, chopped
- 1 tablespoon cornflour
- 1 tablespoon milk
- Salt and pepper, to taste
- 1 (8-count) can organic flaky biscuits
- Oil for misting or cooking spray

Preparation Instructions :

1. In a medium saucepan, bring chicken broth to a boil. Stir in the frozen peas and carrots and cook for 5 minutes over medium heat. Stir in chicken.
2. Mix the cornflour into the milk until it dissolves. Stir it into the simmering chicken broth mixture and cook just until thickened.
3. Remove from heat, add salt and pepper to taste, and let cool slightly.
4. Lay biscuits out on wax paper. Peel each biscuit apart in the middle to make 2 rounds so you have 16 rounds total. Using your hands or a rolling pin, flatten each biscuit round slightly to make it larger and thinner.
5. Divide chicken filling among 8 of the biscuit rounds. Place remaining biscuit rounds on top and press edges all around. Use the tines of a fork to crimp biscuit edges and make sure they are sealed well.
6. Spray both sides lightly with oil or cooking spray.
7. Cook in a single layer, 4 at a time, at 170ºC for 10 minutes or until biscuit dough is cooked through and golden brown.

Sweet Chili Spiced Chicken

Prep time: 10 minutes
Cook time: 43 minutes
Serves 4

Ingredients :

Spice Rub:
- 2 tablespoons brown sugar
- 2 tablespoons paprika
- 1 teaspoon dry mustard powder
- 1 teaspoon chili powder
- 2 tablespoons coarse sea salt or kosher salt
- 2 teaspoons coarsely ground black pepper
- 1 tablespoon vegetable oil
- 1 (1.6 kg) chicken, cut into 8 pieces

Preparation Instructions :

1. Prepare the spice rub by combining the brown sugar, paprika, mustard powder, chili powder, salt and pepper. Rub the oil all over the chicken pieces and then rub the spice mix onto the chicken, covering completely. This is done very easily in a zipper sealable bag. You can do this ahead of time and let the chicken marinate in the refrigerator, or just proceed with cooking right away.
2. Preheat the air fryer to 190ºC.
3. Air fry the chicken in two batches. Place the two chicken thighs and two drumsticks into the air fryer basket. Air fry at 190ºC for 10 minutes. Then, gently turn the chicken pieces over and air fry for another 10 minutes. Remove the chicken pieces and let them rest on a plate while you cook the chicken breasts. Air fry the chicken breasts, skin side down for 8 minutes. Turn the chicken breasts over and air fry for another 12 minutes.
4. Lower the temperature of the air fryer to 170ºC. Place the first batch of chicken on top of the second batch already in the

basket and air fry for a final 3 minutes.

5. Let the chicken rest for 5 minutes and serve warm with some mashed potatoes and a green salad or vegetables.

African Merguez Meatballs

Prep time: 30 minutes
Cook time: 10 minutes
Serves 4

Ingredients :

- 450 g chicken mince
- 2 garlic cloves, finely minced
- 1 tablespoon sweet Hungarian paprika
- 1 teaspoon kosher salt
- 1 teaspoon sugar
- 1 teaspoon ground cumin
- ½ teaspoon black pepper
- ½ teaspoon ground fennel
- ½ teaspoon ground coriander
- ½ teaspoon cayenne pepper
- ¼ teaspoon ground allspice

Preparation Instructions :

1. In a large bowl, gently mix the chicken, garlic, paprika, salt, sugar, cumin, black pepper, fennel, coriander, cayenne, and allspice until all the ingredients are incorporated. Let stand for 30 minutes at room temperature, or cover and refrigerate for up to 24 hours.

2. Form the mixture into 16 meatballs. Arrange them in a single layer in the air fryer basket. Set the air fryer to 200°C for 10 minutes, turning the meatballs halfway through the cooking time. Use a meat thermometer to ensure the meatballs have reached an internal temperature of 76°C.

Thai Chicken with Cucumber and Chili Salad

Prep time: 25 minutes
Cook time: 25 minutes
Serves 6

Ingredients :

- 2 (570 g) small chickens, giblets discarded
- 1 tablespoon fish sauce
- 6 tablespoons chopped fresh coriander
- 2 teaspoons lime zest
- 1 teaspoon ground coriander
- 2 garlic cloves, minced
- 2 tablespoons packed light brown sugar
- 2 teaspoons vegetable oil
- Salt and ground black pepper, to taste
- 1 English cucumber, halved lengthwise and sliced thin
- 1 Thai chili, stemmed, deseeded, and minced
- 2 tablespoons chopped dry-roasted peanuts
- 1 small shallot, sliced thinly
- 1 tablespoon lime juice
- Lime wedges, for serving
- Cooking spray

Preparation Instructions :

1. Arrange a chicken on a clean work surface, remove the backbone with kitchen shears, then pound the chicken breast to flat. Cut the breast in half. Repeat with the remaining chicken.

2. Loose the breast and thigh skin with your fingers, then pat the chickens dry and pierce about 10 holes into the fat deposits of the chickens. Tuck the wings under the chickens.

3. Combine 2 teaspoons of fish sauce, coriander, lime zest, coriander, garlic, 4 teaspoons of sugar, 1 teaspoon of vegetable oil, ½ teaspoon of salt, and ⅛ teaspoon of ground black pepper in a

small bowl. Stir to mix well.

4. Rub the fish sauce mixture under the breast and thigh skin of the game chickens, then let sit for 10 minutes to marinate.

5. Preheat the air fryer to 200ºC. Spritz the air fryer basket with cooking spray.

6. Arrange the marinated chickens in the preheated air fryer, skin side down.

7. Air fry for 15 minutes, then gently turn the game hens over and air fry for 10 more minutes or until the skin is golden brown and the internal temperature of the chickens reads at least 76ºC.

8. Meanwhile, combine all the remaining ingredients, except for the lime wedges, in a large bowl and sprinkle with salt and black pepper. Toss to mix well.

9. Transfer the fried chickens on a large plate, then sit the salad aside and squeeze the lime wedges over before serving.

Golden Chicken Cutlets

Prep time: 15 minutes
Cook time: 15 minutes
Serves 4

Ingredients :

• 2 tablespoons panko breadcrumbs
• 20 g grated Parmesan cheese
• ⅛ tablespoon paprika
• ½ tablespoon garlic powder
• 2 large eggs
• 4 chicken cutlets
• 1 tablespoon parsley
• Salt and ground black pepper, to taste
• Cooking spray

Preparation Instructions :

1. Preheat air fryer to 200ºC. Spritz the air fryer basket with cooking spray.

2. Combine the breadcrumbs, Parmesan,

paprika, garlic powder, salt, and ground black pepper in a large bowl. Stir to mix well. Beat the eggs in a separate bowl.

3. Dredge the chicken cutlets in the beaten eggs, then roll over the breadcrumbs mixture to coat well. Shake the excess off.

4. Transfer the chicken cutlets in the preheated air fryer and spritz with cooking spray.

5. Air fry for 15 minutes or until crispy and golden brown. Flip the cutlets halfway through.

6. Serve with parsley on top.

Fajita Chicken Strips

Prep time: 10 minutes
Cook time: 15 minutes
Serves 4

Ingredients :

• 450 g boneless, skinless chicken tenderloins, cut into strips
• 3 bell peppers, any color, cut into chunks
• 1 onion, cut into chunks
• 1 tablespoon olive oil
• 1 tablespoon fajita seasoning mix
• Cooking spray

Preparation Instructions :

1. Preheat the air fryer to 190ºC.

2. In a large bowl, mix together the chicken, bell peppers, onion, olive oil, and fajita seasoning mix until completely coated.

3. Spray the air fryer basket lightly with cooking spray.

4. Place the chicken and vegetables in the air fryer basket and lightly spray with cooking spray.

5. Air fry for 7 minutes. Shake the basket and air fry for an additional 5 to 8 minutes, until the chicken is cooked through and the veggies are starting to char.

6. Serve warm.

Chicken Jalfrezi

Prep time: 15 minutes
Cook time: 15 minutes
Serves 4

Ingredients :
Chicken:
- 450 g boneless, skinless chicken thighs, cut into 2 or 3 pieces each
- 1 medium onion, chopped
- 1 large green bell pepper, stemmed, seeded, and chopped
- 2 tablespoons olive oil
- 1 teaspoon ground turmeric
- 1 teaspoon garam masala
- 1 teaspoon kosher salt
- ½ to 1 teaspoon cayenne pepper

Sauce:
- 55 g tomato sauce
- 1 tablespoon water
- 1 teaspoon garam masala
- ½ teaspoon kosher salt
- ½ teaspoon cayenne pepper
- Side salad, rice, or naan bread, for serving

Preparation Instructions :

1. For the chicken: In a large bowl, combine the chicken, onion, bell pepper, oil, turmeric, garam masala, salt, and cayenne. Stir and toss until well combined.

2. Place the chicken and vegetables in the air fryer basket. Set the air fryer to 180ºC for 15 minutes, stirring and tossing halfway through the cooking time. Use a meat thermometer to ensure the chicken has reached an internal temperature of 76ºC.

3. Meanwhile, for the sauce: In a small microwave-safe bowl, combine the tomato sauce, water, garam masala, salt, and cayenne. Microwave on high for 1 minute. Remove and stir. Microwave for another minute; set aside.

4. When the chicken is cooked, remove and place chicken and vegetables in a large bowl. Pour the sauce over all. Stir and toss to coat the chicken and vegetables evenly.

5. Serve with rice, naan, or a side salad.

Chicken Nuggets

Prep time: 10 minutes
Cook time: 15 minutes
Serves 4

Ingredients :
- 450 g chicken mince thighs
- 110 g shredded Mozzarella cheese
- 1 large egg, whisked
- ½ teaspoon salt
- ¼ teaspoon dried oregano
- ¼ teaspoon garlic powder

Preparation Instructions :

1. In a large bowl, combine all ingredients. Form mixture into twenty nugget shapes, about 2 tablespoons each.

2. Place nuggets into ungreased air fryer basket, working in batches if needed. Adjust the temperature to (190ºC and air fry for 15 minutes, turning nuggets halfway through cooking. Let cool 5 minutes before serving.

Indian Fennel Chicken

Prep time: 30 minutes
Cook time: 15 minutes
Serves 4

Ingredients :

- 450 g boneless, skinless chicken thighs, cut crosswise into thirds
- 1 yellow onion, cut into 1½-inch-thick slices
- 1 tablespoon coconut oil, melted
- 2 teaspoons minced fresh ginger
- 2 teaspoons minced garlic
- 1 teaspoon smoked paprika
- 1 teaspoon ground fennel
- 1 teaspoon garam masala
- 1 teaspoon ground turmeric
- 1 teaspoon kosher salt
- ½ to 1 teaspoon cayenne pepper
- Vegetable oil spray
- 2 teaspoons fresh lemon juice
- 5 g chopped fresh coriander or parsley

Preparation Instructions :

1. Use a fork to pierce the chicken all over to allow the marinade to penetrate better.
2. In a large bowl, combine the onion, coconut oil, ginger, garlic, paprika, fennel, garam masala, turmeric, salt, and cayenne. Add the chicken, toss to combine, and marinate at room temperature for 30 minutes, or cover and refrigerate for up to 24 hours.
3. Place the chicken and onion in the air fryer basket. (Discard remaining marinade.) Spray with some vegetable oil spray. Set the air fryer to 180°C for 15 minutes. Halfway through the cooking time, remove the basket, spray the chicken and onion with more vegetable oil spray, and toss gently to coat. At the end of the cooking time, use a meat thermometer to ensure the chicken has reached an internal temperature of 76°C.
4. Transfer the chicken and onion to a serving platter. Sprinkle with the lemon juice and coriander and serve.

Mediterranean Stuffed Chicken Breasts

Prep time: 5 minutes
Cook time: 20 to 25 minutes
Serves 4

Ingredients :

- 4 small boneless, skinless chicken breast halves (about 680 g)
- Salt and freshly ground black pepper, to taste
- 115 g goat cheese
- 6 pitted Kalamata olives, coarsely chopped
- Zest of ½ lemon
- 1 teaspoon minced fresh rosemary or ½ teaspoon ground dried rosemary
- 50 g almond meal
- 60 ml balsamic vinegar
- 6 tablespoons unsalted butter

Preparation Instructions :

1. Preheat the air fryer to 180°C.
2. With a boning knife, cut a wide pocket into the thickest part of each chicken breast half, taking care not to cut all the way through. Season the chicken evenly on both sides with salt and freshly ground black pepper.
3. In a small bowl, mix the cheese, olives, lemon zest, and rosemary. Stuff the pockets with the cheese mixture and secure with toothpicks.
4. Place the almond meal in a shallow bowl and dredge the chicken, shaking off the excess. Coat lightly with olive oil spray.
5. Working in batches if necessary, arrange

the chicken breasts in a single layer in the air fryer basket. Pausing halfway through the cooking time to flip the chicken, air fry for 20 to 25 minutes, until a thermometer inserted into the thickest part registers 76°C.

6. While the chicken is baking, prepare the sauce. In a small pan over medium heat, simmer the balsamic vinegar until thick and syrupy, about 5 minutes. Set aside until the chicken is done. When ready to serve, warm the sauce over medium heat and whisk in the butter, 1 tablespoon at a time, until melted and smooth. Season to taste with salt and pepper.

7. Serve the chicken breasts with the sauce drizzled on top.

Hawaiian Huli Huli Chicken

Prep time: 30 minutes
Cook time: 15 minutes
Serves 4

Ingredients :

- 4 boneless, skinless chicken thighs (680 g)
- 1 (230 g) can pineapple chunks in juice, drained, 60 ml juice reserved
- 60 ml soy sauce
- 50 g sugar
- 2 tablespoons ketchup
- 1 tablespoon minced fresh ginger
- 1 tablespoon minced garlic
- 25 g chopped spring onions

Preparation Instructions :

1. Use a fork to pierce the chicken all over to allow the marinade to penetrate better. Place the chicken in a large bowl or large resealable plastic bag.

2. Set the drained pineapple chunks aside. In a small microwave-safe bowl, combine the pineapple juice, soy sauce, sugar,

ketchup, ginger, and garlic. Pour half the sauce over the chicken; toss to coat. Reserve the remaining sauce. Marinate the chicken at room temperature for 30 minutes, or cover and refrigerate for up to 24 hours.

3. Place the chicken in the air fryer basket. (Discard marinade.) Set the air fryer to 180°C for 15 minutes, turning halfway through the cooking time.

4. Meanwhile, microwave the reserved sauce on high for 45 to 60 seconds, stirring every 15 seconds, until the sauce has the consistency of a thick glaze.

5. At the end of the cooking time, use a meat thermometer to ensure the chicken has reached an internal temperature of 76°C.

6. Transfer the chicken to a serving platter. Pour the sauce over the chicken. Garnish with the pineapple chunks and spring onions.

Crispy Dill Chicken Strips

Prep time: 30 minutes
Cook time: 10 minutes
Serves 4

Ingredients :

- 2 whole boneless, skinless chicken breasts (about 450 g each), halved lengthwise
- 230 ml Italian dressing
- 110 g finely crushed crisps
- 1 tablespoon dried dill weed
- 1 tablespoon garlic powder
- 1 large egg, beaten
- 1 to 2 tablespoons oil

Preparation Instructions :

1. In a large resealable bag, combine the chicken and Italian dressing. Seal the bag and refrigerate to marinate at least 1 hour.

2. In a shallow dish, stir together the potato

chips, dill, and garlic powder. Place the beaten egg in a second shallow dish.

3. Remove the chicken from the marinade. Roll the chicken pieces in the egg and the crisp mixture, coating thoroughly.

4. Preheat the air fryer to 170°C. Line the air fryer basket with parchment paper.

5. Place the coated chicken on the parchment and spritz with oil.

6. Cook for 5 minutes. Flip the chicken, spritz it with oil, and cook for 5 minutes more until the outsides are crispy and the insides are no longer pink.

Ranch Chicken Wings

Prep time: 10 minutes
Cook time: 40 minutes
Serves 4

Ingredients :

- 2 tablespoons water
- 2 tablespoons hot pepper sauce
- 2 tablespoons unsalted butter, melted
- 2 tablespoons apple cider vinegar
- 1 (30 g) envelope ranch salad dressing mix
- 1 teaspoon paprika
- 4 1.8 kg chicken wings, tips removed
- Cooking oil spray

Preparation Instructions :

1. In a large bowl, whisk the water, hot pepper sauce, melted butter, vinegar, salad dressing mix, and paprika until combined.

2. Add the wings and toss to coat. At this point, you can cover the bowl and marinate the wings in the refrigerator for 4 to 24 hours for best results. However, you can just let the wings stand for 30 minutes in the refrigerator.

3. Insert the crisper plate into the basket and the basket into the unit. Preheat the unit by selecting AIR FRY, setting the

temperature to 200°C, and setting the time to 3 minutes. Select START/STOP to begin.

4. Once the unit is preheated, spray the crisper plate with cooking oil. Working in batches, put half the wings into the basket; it is okay to stack them. Refrigerate the remaining wings.

5. Select AIR FRY, set the temperature to 200°C, and set the time to 20 minutes. Select START/STOP to begin.

6. After 5 minutes, remove the basket and shake it. Reinsert the basket to resume cooking. Remove and shake the basket every 5 minutes, three more times, until the chicken is browned and glazed and a food thermometer inserted into the wings registers 76°C.

7. Repeat steps 4, 5, and 6 with the remaining wings.

8. When the cooking is complete, serve warm.

Personal Cauliflower Pizzas

Prep time: 10 minutes
Cook time: 25 minutes
Serves 2

Ingredients :

- 1 (340 g) bag frozen riced cauliflower
- 75 g shredded Mozzarella cheese
- 25 g almond flour
- 20 g Parmesan cheese
- 1 large egg
- ½ teaspoon salt
- 1 teaspoon garlic powder
- 1 teaspoon dried oregano
- 4 tablespoons no-sugar-added marinara sauce, divided
- 110 g fresh Mozzarella, chopped, divided
- 140 g cooked chicken breast, chopped, divided
- 100 g chopped cherry tomatoes, divided
- 5 g fresh baby rocket, divided

Preparation Instructions :

1. Preheat the air fryer to 200ºC. Cut 4 sheets of parchment paper to fit the basket of the air fryer. Brush with olive oil and set aside.

2. In a large glass bowl, microwave the cauliflower according to package directions. Place the cauliflower on a clean towel, draw up the sides, and squeeze tightly over a sink to remove the excess moisture. Return the cauliflower to the bowl and add the shredded Mozzarella along with the almond flour, Parmesan, egg, salt, garlic powder, and oregano. Stir until thoroughly combined.

3. Divide the dough into two equal portions. Place one piece of dough on the prepared parchment paper and pat gently into a thin, flat disk 7 to 8 inches in diameter. Air fry for 15 minutes until the crust begins to brown. Let cool for 5 minutes.

4. Transfer the parchment paper with the crust on top to a baking sheet. Place a second sheet of parchment paper over the crust. While holding the edges of both sheets together, carefully lift the crust off the baking sheet, flip it, and place it back in the air fryer basket. The new sheet of parchment paper is now on the bottom. Remove the top piece of paper and air fry the crust for another 15 minutes until the top begins to brown. Remove the basket from the air fryer.

5. Spread 2 tablespoons of the marinara sauce on top of the crust, followed by half the fresh Mozzarella, chicken, cherry tomatoes, and rocket. Air fry for 5 to 10 minutes longer, until the cheese is melted and beginning to brown. Remove the pizza from the oven and let it sit for 10 minutes before serving. Repeat with the remaining ingredients to make a second pizza.

Breaded Turkey Cutlets

Prep time: 5 minutes
Cook time: 8 minutes
Serves 4

Ingredients :

- 60 g whole wheat bread crumbs
- ¼ teaspoon paprika
- ¼ teaspoon salt
- ¼ teaspoon black pepper
- ⅛ teaspoon dried sage
- ⅛ teaspoon garlic powder
- 1 egg
- 4 turkey breast cutlets
- Chopped fresh parsley, for serving

Preparation Instructions :

1. Preheat the air fryer to 192ºC.

2. In a medium shallow bowl, whisk together the bread crumbs, paprika, salt, black pepper, sage, and garlic powder.

3. In a separate medium shallow bowl, whisk the egg until frothy.

4. Dip each turkey cutlet into the egg mixture, then into the bread crumb mixture, coating the outside with the crumbs. Place the breaded turkey cutlets in a single layer in the bottom of the air fryer basket, making sure that they don't touch each other.

5. Bake for 4 minutes. Turn the cutlets over, then bake for 4 minutes more, or until the internal temperature reaches 76ºC. Sprinkle on the parsley and serve.

Crunchy Chicken with Roasted Carrots

Prep time: 10 minutes
Cook time: 22 minutes
Serves 4

Ingredients :

- 4 bone-in, skin-on chicken thighs
- 2 carrots, cut into 2-inch pieces
- 2 tablespoons extra-virgin olive oil
- 2 teaspoons poultry spice
- 1 teaspoon sea salt, divided
- 2 teaspoons chopped fresh rosemary leaves
- Cooking oil spray
- 500 g cooked white rice

Preparation Instructions :

1. Brush the chicken thighs and carrots with olive oil. Sprinkle both with the poultry spice, salt, and rosemary.
2. Insert the crisper plate into the basket and the basket into the unit. Preheat the unit by selecting AIR FRY, setting the temperature to 200ºC, and setting the time to 3 minutes. Select START/STOP to begin.
3. Once the unit is preheated, spray the crisper plate with cooking oil. Place the carrots into the basket. Add the wire rack and arrange the chicken thighs on the rack.
4. Select AIR FRY, set the temperature to 200ºC, and set the time to 20 minutes. Select START/STOP to begin.
5. When the cooking is complete, check the chicken temperature. If a food thermometer inserted into the chicken registers 76ºC, remove the chicken from the air fryer, place it on a clean plate, and cover with aluminum foil to keep warm. Otherwise, resume cooking for 1 to 2 minutes longer.
6. The carrots can cook for 18 to 22 minutes and will be tender and caramelized; cooking time isn't as crucial for root vegetables.
7. Serve the chicken and carrots with the hot cooked rice.

Polenta Casserole

Prep time: 5 minutes
Cook time: 28 to 30 minutes
Serves 4

Ingredients :

- 10 fresh asparagus spears, cut into 1-inch pieces
- 320 g cooked polenta, cooled to room temperature
- 1 egg, beaten
- 2 teaspoons Worcestershire sauce
- ½ teaspoon garlic powder
- ¼ teaspoon salt
- 2 slices emmental cheese (about 40 g)
- Oil for misting or cooking spray

Preparation Instructions :

1. Mist asparagus spears with oil and air fry at 200ºC for 5 minutes, until crisp-tender.
2. In a medium bowl, mix together the grits, egg, Worcestershire, garlic powder, and salt.
3. Spoon half of polenta mixture into a baking pan and top with asparagus.
4. Tear cheese slices into pieces and layer evenly on top of asparagus.
5. Top with remaining polenta.
6. Bake at 180ºC for 23 to 25 minutes. The casserole will rise a little as it cooks. When done, the top will have browned lightly with just a hint of crispiness.

Zesty Fried Asparagus

Prep time: 3 minutes
Cook time: 10 minutes
Serves 4

Ingredients :

- Oil, for spraying
- 10 to 12 spears asparagus, trimmed
- 2 tablespoons olive oil
- 1 tablespoon garlic powder
- 1 teaspoon chili powder
- ½ teaspoon ground cumin
- ¼ teaspoon salt

Preparation Instructions :

1. Line the air fryer basket with parchment and spray lightly with oil.
2. If the asparagus are too long to fit easily in the air fryer, cut them in half.
3. Place the asparagus, olive oil, garlic, chili powder, cumin, and salt in a zip-top plastic bag, seal, and toss until evenly coated.
4. Place the asparagus in the prepared basket.
5. Roast at 200ºC for 5 minutes, flip, and cook for another 5 minutes, or until bright green and firm but tender.

Curried Fruit

Prep time: 10 minutes
Cook time: 20 minutes
Serves 6 to 8

Ingredients :

- 210 g cubed fresh pineapple
- 200 g cubed fresh pear (firm, not overly ripe)
- 230 g frozen peaches, thawed
- 425 g can dark, sweet, pitted cherries with juice
- 2 tablespoons brown sugar
- 1 teaspoon curry powder

Preparation Instructions :

1. Combine all ingredients in large bowl. Stir gently to mix in the sugar and curry.
2. Pour into a baking pan and bake at 180°C for 10 minutes.
3. Stir fruit and cook 10 more minutes.
4. Serve hot.

Super Cheesy Gold Aubergine

Prep time: 15 minutes
Cook time: 30 minutes
Serves 4

Ingredients :

- 1 medium aubergine, peeled and cut into ½-inch-thick rounds
- 1 teaspoon salt, plus more for seasoning
- 60 g plain flour
- 2 eggs
- 90 g Italian bread crumbs
- 2 tablespoons grated Parmesan cheese
- Freshly ground black pepper, to taste
- Cooking oil spray
- 180 g marinara sauce
- 45 g shredded Parmesan cheese, divided
- 110 g shredded Mozzarella cheese, divided

Preparation Instructions :

1. Blot the aubergine with paper towels to dry completely. You can also sprinkle with 1 teaspoon of salt to sweat out the moisture; if you do this, rinse the aubergine slices and blot dry again.
2. Place the flour in a shallow bowl.
3. In another shallow bowl, beat the eggs.
4. In a third shallow bowl, stir together the bread crumbs and grated Parmesan cheese and season with salt and pepper.
5. Dip each aubergine round in the flour, in the eggs, and into the bread crumbs to coat.
6. Insert the crisper plate into the basket and the basket into the unit. Preheat the unit by selecting AIR FRY, setting the temperature to 200°C, and setting the time to 3 minutes. Select START/STOP to begin.
7. Once the unit is preheated, spray the crisper plate and the basket with cooking oil. Working in batches, place the aubergine rounds into the basket. Do not stack them. Spray the aubergine with the cooking oil.
8. Select AIR FRY, set the temperature to 200°C, and set the time to 10 minutes. Select START/STOP to begin.
9. After 7 minutes, open the unit and top each round with 1 teaspoon of marinara sauce and ½ tablespoon each of shredded Parmesan and Mozzarella cheese. Resume cooking for 2 to 3 minutes until the cheese melts.
10. Repeat steps 5, 6, 7, 8, and 9 with the remaining aubergine.
11. When the cooking is complete, serve immediately.

Flatbread

Prep time: 5 minutes
Cook time: 7 minutes
Serves 2

Ingredients :

- 225 g shredded Mozzarella cheese
- 25 g blanched finely ground almond flour
- 30 g full-fat cream cheese, softened

Preparation Instructions :

1. In a large microwave-safe bowl, melt Mozzarella in the microwave for 30 seconds. Stir in almond flour until smooth and then add cream cheese. Continue mixing until dough forms, gently kneading it with wet hands if necessary.
2. Divide the dough into two pieces and roll out to ¼-inch thickness between two pieces of parchment. Cut another piece of parchment to fit your air fryer basket.
3. Place a piece of flatbread onto your parchment and into the air fryer, working in two batches if needed.
4. Adjust the temperature to 160ºC and air fry for 7 minutes.
5. Halfway through the cooking time flip the flatbread. Serve warm.

Burger Bun for One

Prep time: 2 minutes
Cook time: 5 minutes
Serves 1

Ingredients :

- 2 tablespoons salted butter, melted
- 25 g blanched finely ground almond flour
- ¼ teaspoon baking powder
- ⅛ teaspoon apple cider vinegar
- 1 large egg, whisked

Preparation Instructions :

1. Pour butter into an ungreased ramekin. Add flour, baking powder, and vinegar to ramekin and stir until combined. Add egg and stir until batter is mostly smooth.
2. Place ramekin into air fryer basket. Adjust the temperature to 180ºC and bake for 5 minutes. When done, the centre will be firm and the top slightly browned. Let cool, about 5 minutes, then remove from ramekin and slice in half. Serve.

Roasted Aubergine

Prep time: 15 minutes
Cook time: 15 minutes
Serves 4

Ingredients :

- 1 large aubergine
- 2 tablespoons olive oil
- ¼ teaspoon salt
- ½ teaspoon garlic powder

Preparation Instructions :

1. Remove top and bottom from aubergine. Slice aubergine into ¼-inch-thick round slices.
2. Brush slices with olive oil. Sprinkle with salt and garlic powder. Place aubergine slices into the air fryer basket.
3. Adjust the temperature to 200ºCand set the timer for 15 minutes.
4. Serve immediately.

Scalloped Potatoes

Prep time: 5 minutes
Cook time: 20 minutes
Serves 4

Ingredients :

- 440 g sliced frozen potatoes, thawed
- 3 cloves garlic, minced
- Pinch salt
- Freshly ground black pepper, to taste
- 180 g double cream

Preparation Instructions :

1. Preheat the air fryer to 192°C.
2. Toss the potatoes with the garlic, salt, and black pepper in a baking pan until evenly coated. Pour the double cream over the top.
3. Place the baking pan in the air fryer basket and bake for 15 minutes, or until the potatoes are tender and top is golden brown. Check for doneness and bake for another 5 minutes as needed.
4. Serve hot.

Blackened Courgette with Kimchi-Herb Sauce

Prep time: 10 minutes
Cook time: 15 minutes
Serves 2

Ingredients :

- 2 medium courgettes, ends trimmed (about 170 g each)
- 2 tablespoons olive oil
- 75 g kimchi, finely chopped
- 5 g finely chopped fresh coriander
- 5 g finely chopped fresh flat-leaf parsley, plus more for garnish
- 2 tablespoons rice vinegar
- 2 teaspoons Asian chili-garlic sauce
- 1 teaspoon grated fresh ginger
- coarse sea salt and freshly ground black pepper, to taste

Preparation Instructions :

1. Brush the courgettes with half of the olive oil, place in the air fryer, and air fry at 200°C, turning halfway through, until lightly charred on the outside and tender, about 15 minutes.
2. Meanwhile, in a small bowl, combine the remaining 1 tablespoon olive oil, the kimchi, coriander, parsley, vinegar, chili-garlic sauce, and ginger.
3. Once the courgette is finished cooking, transfer it to a colander and let it cool for 5 minutes. Using your fingers, pinch and break the courgette into bite-size pieces, letting them fall back into the colander. Season the courgette with salt and pepper, toss to combine, then let sit a further 5 minutes to allow some of its liquid to drain. Pile the courgette atop the kimchi sauce on a plate and sprinkle with more parsley to serve.

Roasted Potatoes and Asparagus

Prep time: 5 minutes
Cook time: 23 minutes
Serves 4

Ingredients :

- 4 medium potatoes
- 1 bunch asparagus
- 75 g cottage cheese
- 80 g low-fat crème fraiche
- 1 tablespoon wholegrain mustard
- Salt and pepper, to taste
- Cooking spray

Preparation Instructions :

1. Preheat the air fryer to 200°C. Spritz the

air fryer basket with cooking spray.

2. Place the potatoes in the basket. Air fry the potatoes for 20 minutes.
3. Boil the asparagus in salted water for 3 minutes.
4. Remove the potatoes and mash them with rest of ingredients. Sprinkle with salt and pepper.
5. Serve immediately.

Lemon-Thyme Asparagus

Prep time: 5 minutes
Cook time: 4 to 8 minutes
Serves 4

Ingredients :

- 450 g asparagus, woody ends trimmed off
- 1 tablespoon avocado oil
- ½ teaspoon dried thyme or ½ tablespoon chopped fresh thyme
- Sea salt and freshly ground black pepper, to taste
- 60 g goat cheese, crumbled
- Zest and juice of 1 lemon
- Flaky sea salt, for serving (optional)

Preparation Instructions :

1. In a medium bowl, toss together the asparagus, avocado oil, and thyme, and season with sea salt and pepper.
2. Place the asparagus in the air fryer basket in a single layer. Set the air fryer to 200°C and air fry for 4 to 8 minutes, to your desired doneness.
3. Transfer to a serving platter. Top with the goat cheese, lemon zest, and lemon juice. If desired, season with a pinch of flaky salt.

Courgette Fritters

Prep time: 10 minutes
Cook time: 10 minutes
Serves 4

Ingredients :

- 2 courgette, grated (about 450 g)
- 1 teaspoon salt
- 25 g almond flour
- 20 g grated Parmesan cheese
- 1 large egg
- ¼ teaspoon dried thyme
- ¼ teaspoon ground turmeric
- ¼ teaspoon freshly ground black pepper
- 1 tablespoon olive oil
- ½ lemon, sliced into wedges

Preparation Instructions :

1. Preheat the air fryer to 200°C. Cut a piece of parchment paper to fit slightly smaller than the bottom of the air fryer.
2. Place the courgette in a large colander and sprinkle with the salt. Let sit for 5 to 10 minutes. Squeeze as much liquid as you can from the courgette and place in a large mixing bowl. Add the almond flour, Parmesan, egg, thyme, turmeric, and black pepper. Stir gently until thoroughly combined.
3. Shape the mixture into 8 patties and arrange on the parchment paper. Brush lightly with the olive oil. Pausing halfway through the cooking time to turn the patties, air fry for 10 minutes until golden brown. Serve warm with the lemon wedges.

Sesame Taj Tofu

Prep time: 5 minutes
Cook time: 25 minutes
Serves 4

Ingredients :

- 1 block firm tofu, pressed and cut into 1-inch thick cubes
- 2 tablespoons soy sauce
- 2 teaspoons toasted sesame seeds
- 1 teaspoon rice vinegar
- 1 tablespoon cornflour

Preparation Instructions :

1. Preheat the air fryer to 200°C.
2. Add the tofu, soy sauce, sesame seeds, and rice vinegar in a bowl together and mix well to coat the tofu cubes. Then cover the tofu in cornflour and put it in the air fryer basket.
3. Air fry for 25 minutes, giving the basket a shake at five-minute intervals to ensure the tofu cooks evenly.
4. Serve immediately.

Fig, Chickpea, and Rocket Salad

Prep time: 15 minutes
Cook time: 20 minutes
Serves 4

Ingredients :

- 8 fresh figs, halved
- 250 g cooked chickpeas
- 1 teaspoon crushed roasted cumin seeds
- 4 tablespoons balsamic vinegar
- 2 tablespoons extra-virgin olive oil, plus more for greasing
- Salt and ground black pepper, to taste
- 40 g rocket, washed and dried

Preparation Instructions :

1. Preheat the air fryer to 192°C.
2. Cover the air fryer basket with aluminum foil and grease lightly with oil. Put the figs in the air fryer basket and air fry for 10 minutes.
3. In a bowl, combine the chickpeas and cumin seeds.
4. Remove the air fried figs from the air fryer and replace with the chickpeas. Air fry for 10 minutes. Leave to cool.
5. In the meantime, prepare the dressing. Mix the balsamic vinegar, olive oil, salt and pepper.
6. In a salad bowl, combine the rocket with the cooled figs and chickpeas.
7. Toss with the sauce and serve.

Dinner Rolls

Prep time: 10 minutes
Cook time: 12 minutes
Serves 6

Ingredients :

- 225 g shredded Mozzarella cheese
- 30 g full-fat cream cheese
- 95 g blanched finely ground almond flour
- 40 g ground flaxseed
- ½ teaspoon baking powder
- 1 large egg

Preparation Instructions :

1. Place Mozzarella, cream cheese, and almond flour in a large microwave-safe bowl. Microwave for 1 minute. Mix until smooth.
2. Add flaxseed, baking powder, and egg until fully combined and smooth. Microwave an additional 15 seconds if it becomes too firm.
3. Separate the dough into six pieces and roll into balls. Place the balls into the air

fryer basket.

4. Adjust the temperature to 160°C and air fry for 12 minutes.

5. Allow rolls to cool completely before serving.

Hawaiian Brown Rice

Prep time: 10 minutes
Cook time: 12 to 16 minutes
Serves 4 to 6

Ingredients :

- 110 g ground sausage
- 1 teaspoon butter
- 20 g minced onion
- 40 g minced bell pepper
- 380 g cooked brown rice
- 1 (230 g) can crushed pineapple, drained

Preparation Instructions :

1. Shape sausage into 3 or 4 thin patties. Air fry at 200°C for 6 to 8 minutes or until well done. Remove from air fryer, drain, and crumble. Set aside.

2. Place butter, onion, and bell pepper in baking pan. Roast at 200°C for 1 minute and stir. Cook 3 to 4 minutes longer or just until vegetables are tender.

3. Add sausage, rice, and pineapple to vegetables and stir together.

4. Roast for 2 to 3 minutes, until heated through.

Sesame Carrots and Sugar Snap Peas

Prep time: 10 minutes
Cook time: 16 minutes
Serves 4

Ingredients :

- 450 g carrots, peeled sliced on the bias (½-inch slices)
- 1 teaspoon olive oil
- Salt and freshly ground black pepper, to taste
- 110 g honey
- 1 tablespoon sesame oil
- 1 tablespoon soy sauce
- ½ teaspoon minced fresh ginger
- 110 g sugar snap peas
- 1½ teaspoons sesame seeds

Preparation Instructions :

1. Preheat the air fryer to 180°C.

2. Toss the carrots with the olive oil, season with salt and pepper and air fry for 10 minutes, shaking the basket once or twice during the cooking process.

3. Combine the honey, sesame oil, soy sauce and minced ginger in a large bowl. Add the sugar snap peas and the air-fried carrots to the honey mixture, toss to coat and return everything to the air fryer basket.

4. Turn up the temperature to 200°C and air fry for an additional 6 minutes, shaking the basket once during the cooking process.

5. Transfer the carrots and sugar snap peas to a serving bowl. Pour the sauce from the bottom of the cooker over the vegetables and sprinkle sesame seeds over top. Serve immediately.

Parmesan Mushrooms

Prep time: 5 minutes
Cook time: 15 minutes
Serves 4

Ingredients :

- Oil, for spraying
- 450 g shitake mushrooms, stems trimmed
- 2 tablespoons olive oil
- 2 teaspoons granulated garlic
- 1 teaspoon onion powder
- ½ teaspoon salt
- ¼ teaspoon freshly ground black pepper
- 30 g grated Parmesan cheese, divided

Preparation Instructions :

1. Line the air fryer basket with parchment and spray lightly with oil.
2. In a large bowl, toss the mushrooms with the olive oil, garlic, onion powder, salt, and black pepper until evenly coated.
3. Place the mushrooms in the prepared basket.
4. Roast at 192ºC for 13 minutes.
5. Sprinkle half of the cheese over the mushrooms and cook for another 2 minutes.
6. Transfer the mushrooms to a serving bowl, add the remaining Parmesan cheese, and toss until evenly coated. Serve immediately.

Maple-Roasted Tomatoes

Prep time: 15 minutes
Cook time: 20 minutes
Serves 2

Ingredients :

- 280 g cherry tomatoes, halved
- coarse sea salt, to taste
- 2 tablespoons maple syrup
- 1 tablespoon vegetable oil
- 2 sprigs fresh thyme, stems removed
- 1 garlic clove, minced
- Freshly ground black pepper

Preparation Instructions :

1. Place the tomatoes in a colander and sprinkle liberally with salt. Let stand for 10 minutes to drain.
2. Transfer the tomatoes cut-side up to a cake pan, then drizzle with the maple syrup, followed by the oil. Sprinkle with the thyme leaves and garlic and season with pepper. Place the pan in the air fryer and roast at 160ºC until the tomatoes are soft, collapsed, and lightly caramelized on top, about 20 minutes.
3. Serve straight from the pan or transfer the tomatoes to a plate and drizzle with the juices from the pan to serve.

Garlic and Thyme Tomatoes

Prep time: 10 minutes
Cook time: 15 minutes
Serves 2 to 4

Ingredients :

- 4 plum tomatoes
- 1 tablespoon olive oil
- Salt and freshly ground black pepper, to taste
- 1 clove garlic, minced
- ½ teaspoon dried thyme

Preparation Instructions :

1. Preheat the air fryer to 200ºC.
2. Cut the tomatoes in half and scoop out the seeds and any pithy parts with your fingers. Place the tomatoes in a bowl and toss with the olive oil, salt, pepper, garlic and thyme.
3. Transfer the tomatoes to the air fryer, cut side up. Air fry for 15 minutes. The edges should just start to brown. Let the tomatoes cool to an edible temperature for a few minutes and then use in pastas, on top of crostini, or as an accompaniment to any poultry, meat or fish.

Chapter 9 Desserts

Air Fryer Apple Fritters

Prep time: 30 minutes
Cook time: 7 to 8 minutes
Serves 6

Ingredients :

- 1 chopped, peeled Granny Smith apple
- 115 g granulated sugar
- 1 teaspoon ground cinnamon
- 120 g plain flour
- 1 teaspoon baking powder
- 1 teaspoon salt
- 2 tablespoons milk
- 2 tablespoons butter, melted
- 1 large egg, beaten
- Cooking spray
- 25 g icing sugar (optional)

Preparation Instructions :

1. Mix together the apple, granulated sugar, and cinnamon in a small bowl. Allow to sit for 30 minutes.
2. Combine the flour, baking powder, and salt in a medium bowl. Add the milk, butter, and egg and stir to incorporate.
3. Pour the apple mixture into the bowl of flour mixture and stir with a spatula until a dough forms.
4. Make the fritters: On a clean work surface, divide the dough into 12 equal portions and shape into 1-inch balls. Flatten them into patties with your hands.
5. Preheat the air fryer to 176°C. Line the air fryer basket with baking paper and spray it with cooking spray.
6. Transfer the apple fritters onto the baking paper, evenly spaced but not too close together. Spray the fritters with cooking spray.
7. Bake for 7 to 8 minutes until lightly browned. Flip the fritters halfway through the cooking time.
8. Remove from the basket to a plate and serve with the confectioners' sugar sprinkled on top, if desired.

Baked Peaches with Yogurt and Blueberries

Prep time: 10 minutes
Cook time: 7 to 11 minutes
Serves 6

Ingredients :

- 3 peaches, peeled, halved, and pitted
- 2 tablespoons packed brown sugar
- 285 g plain Greek yogurt
- ¼ teaspoon ground cinnamon
- 1 teaspoon pure vanilla extract
- 190 g fresh blueberries

Preparation Instructions :

1. Preheat the air fryer to 192°C.
2. Arrange the peaches in the air fryer basket, cut side up. Top with a generous sprinkle of brown sugar.
3. Bake in the preheated air fryer for 7 to 11 minutes, or until the peaches are lightly browned and caramelized.
4. Meanwhile, whisk together the yogurt, cinnamon, and vanilla in a small bowl until smooth.
5. Remove the peaches from the basket to a plate. Serve topped with the yogurt mixture and fresh blueberries.

Baked Apples and Walnuts

Prep time: 6 minutes
Cook time: 20 minutes
Serves 4

Ingredients :

- 4 small Granny Smith apples
- 50 g chopped walnuts
- 50 g light brown sugar
- 2 tablespoons butter, melted
- 1 teaspoon ground cinnamon
- ½ teaspoon ground nutmeg
- 120 ml water, or apple juice

Preparation Instructions :

1. Cut off the top third of the apples. Spoon out the core and some of the flesh and discard. Place the apples in a small air fryer baking pan.
2. Insert the crisper plate into the basket and the basket into the unit. Preheat to 176°C.
3. In a small bowl, stir together the walnuts, brown sugar, melted butter, cinnamon, and nutmeg. Spoon this mixture into the centers of the hollowed-out apples.
4. Once the unit is preheated, pour the water into the crisper plate. Place the baking pan into the basket.
5. Bake for 20 minutes.
6. When the cooking is complete, the apples should be bubbly and fork tender.

Kentucky Chocolate Nut Pie

Prep time: 20 minutes
Cook time: 25 minutes
Serves 8

Ingredients :

- 2 large eggs, beaten
- 75 g unsalted butter, melted
- 200 g granulated sugar
- 60 g plain flour

- 190 g coarsely chopped pecans
- 170 g milk chocolate chips
- 2 tablespoons bourbon, or peach juice
- 1 (9-inch) unbaked piecrust

Preparation Instructions :

1. In a large bowl, stir together the eggs and melted butter. Add the sugar and flour and stir until combined. Stir in the pecans, chocolate chips, and bourbon until well mixed.
2. Using a fork, prick holes in the bottom and sides of the pie crust. Pour the pie filling into the crust.
3. Preheat the air fryer to 176°C.
4. Cook for 25 minutes, or until a knife inserted into the middle of the pie comes out clean. Let set for 5 minutes before serving.

Baked Apple

Prep time: 10 minutes
Cook time: 20 minutes
Makes 6 apple halves

Ingredients :

- 3 small Pink Lady or other baking apples
- 3 tablespoons maple syrup
- 3 tablespoons chopped pecans
- 1 tablespoon firm butter, cut into 6 pieces

Preparation Instructions :

1. Put 6.5 tablespoons water in the drawer of the air fryer.
2. Wash apples well and dry them.
3. Split apples in half. Remove core and a little of the flesh to make a cavity for the pecans.
4. Place apple halves in air fryer basket, cut side up.
5. Spoon 1½ teaspoons pecans into each cavity.

6. Spoon ½ tablespoon maple syrup over pecans in each apple.

7. Top each apple with 1 piece of butter.

8. Bake at 184ºC for 20 minutes, until apples are tender.

Brown Sugar Banana Bread

Prep time: 20 minutes
Cook time: 22 to 24 minutes
Serves 4

Ingredients :

- 195 g packed light brown sugar
- 1 large egg, beaten
- 2 tablespoons unsalted butter, melted
- 120 ml milk, whole or semi-skimmed
- 250 g plain flour
- 1½ teaspoons baking powder
- 1 teaspoon ground cinnamon
- ½ teaspoon salt
- 1 banana, mashed
- 1 to 2 tablespoons coconut, or avocado oil oil
- 30 g icing sugar (optional)

Preparation Instructions :

1. In a large bowl, stir together the brown sugar, egg, melted butter, and milk.

2. In a medium bowl, whisk the flour, baking powder, cinnamon, and salt until blended. Add the flour mixture to the sugar mixture and stir just to blend.

3. Add the mashed banana and stir to combine.

4. Preheat the air fryer to 176ºC. Spritz 2 mini loaf pans with oil.

5. Evenly divide the batter between the prepared pans and place them in the air fryer basket.

6. Cook for 22 to 24 minutes, or until a knife inserted into the middle of the loaves comes out clean.

7. Dust the warm loaves with icing sugar (if using).

Mini Cheesecake

Prep time: 10 minutes
Cook time: 15 minutes
Serves 2

Ingredients :

- 50 g walnuts
- 2 tablespoons salted butter
- 2 tablespoons granulated sweetener
- 110 g full-fat cream cheese, softened
- 1 large egg
- ½ teaspoon vanilla extract
- 35 g powdered sweetener

Preparation Instructions :

1. Place walnuts, butter, and granulated sweetener in a food processor. Pulse until ingredients stick together and a dough forms.

2. Press dough into a springform pan then place the pan into the air fryer basket.

3. Adjust the temperature to 204ºC and bake for 5 minutes.

4. When done, remove the crust and let cool.

5. In a medium bowl, mix cream cheese with egg, vanilla extract, and powdered sweetener until smooth.

6. Spoon mixture on top of baked walnut crust and place into the air fryer basket.

7. Adjust the temperature to 148ºC and bake for 10 minutes.

8. Once done, chill for 2 hours before serving.

Berry Crumble

Prep time: 10 minutes
Cook time: 15 minutes
Serves 4

Ingredients :

- For the Filling:
- 300 g mixed berries
- 2 tablespoons sugar
- 1 tablespoon cornflour
- 1 tablespoon fresh lemon juice
- For the Topping
- 30 g plain flour
- 20 g rolled oats
- 1 tablespoon granulated sugar
- 2 tablespoons cold unsalted butter, cut into small cubes
- Whipped cream or ice cream (optional)

Preparation Instructions :

1. Preheat the air fryer to 204°C.
2. For the filling: In a round baking pan, gently mix the berries, sugar, cornflour, and lemon juice until thoroughly combined.
3. For the topping: In a small bowl, combine the flour, oats, and sugar. Stir the butter into the flour mixture until the mixture has the consistency of breadcrumbs.
4. Sprinkle the topping over the berries.
5. Put the pan in the air fryer basket and air fry for 15 minutes. Let cool for 5 minutes on a wire rack.
6. Serve topped with whipped cream or ice cream, if desired.

Pecan Bars

Prep time: 5 minutes
Cook time: 40 minutes
Serves 12

Ingredients :

- 220 g coconut flour
- 5 tablespoons granulated sweetener
- 4 tablespoons coconut oil, softened
- 60 ml heavy cream
- 1 egg, beaten
- 4 pecans, chopped

Preparation Instructions :

1. Mix coconut flour, sweetener, coconut oil, heavy cream, and egg.
2. Pour the batter in the air fryer basket and flatten well.
3. Top the mixture with pecans and cook the meal at 176°C for 40 minutes.
4. Cut the cooked meal into the bars.

Tortilla Fried Hand Pies

Prep time: 10 minutes
Cook time: 5 minutes per batch
Makes 12 pies

Ingredients :

- 12 small flour tortillas (4-inch diameter)
- 160 g fig jam
- 20 g slivered almonds
- 2 tablespoons desiccated, unsweetened coconut
- Coconut, or avocado oil for misting or cooking spray

Preparation Instructions :

1. Wrap refrigerated tortillas in damp paper towels and heat in microwave 30 seconds to warm.
2. Working with one tortilla at a time, place 2 teaspoons fig jam, 1 teaspoon slivered

almonds, and ½ teaspoon coconut in the center of each.

3. Moisten outer edges of tortilla all around.

4. Fold one side of tortilla over filling, to make a half-moon shape, and press down lightly on center. Using the tines of a fork, press down firmly on edges of tortilla to seal in filling.

5. Mist both sides with oil or cooking spray.

6. Place hand pies in air fryer basket, close, but not overlapping. It's fine to lean some against the sides and corners of the basket. You may need to cook in 2 batches.

7. Air fry at 200ºC for 5 minutes, or until lightly browned. Serve hot.

8. Refrigerate any leftover pies in a closed container. To serve later, toss them back in the air fryer basket and cook for 2 to 3 minutes to reheat.

Maple-Pecan Tart with Sea Salt

Prep time: 15 minutes
Cook time: 25 minutes
Serves 8

Ingredients :

Tart Crust:
Vegetable oil spray
- 75 g unsalted butter, softened
- 50 g firmly packed brown sugar
- 125 g plain flour
- ¼ teaspoon kosher, or coarse sea salt

Filling:
- 4 tablespoons unsalted butter, diced
- 95 g packed brown sugar
- 60 ml pure maple syrup
- 60 ml whole milk
- ¼ teaspoon pure vanilla extract
- 190 g finely chopped pecans
- ¼ teaspoon flaked sea salt

Preparation Instructions :

1. For the crust: Line a baking pan with foil, leaving a couple of inches of overhang. Spray the foil with vegetable oil spray.

2. In a medium bowl, combine the butter and brown sugar. Beat with an electric mixer on medium-low speed until light and fluffy. Add the flour and kosher salt and beat until the ingredients are well blended. Transfer the mixture (it will be crumbly) to the prepared pan. Press it evenly into the bottom of the pan.

3. Place the pan in the air fryer basket. Set the air fryer to 176ºC and cook for 13 minutes. When the crust has 5 minutes left to cook, start the filling.

4. For the filling: In a medium saucepan, combine the butter, brown sugar, maple syrup, and milk. Bring to a simmer, stirring occasionally. When it begins simmering, cook for 1 minute. Remove from the heat and stir in the vanilla and pecans.

5. Carefully pour the filling evenly over the crust, gently spreading with a rubber spatula so the nuts and liquid are evenly distributed. Keep the air fryer at 176ºC and cook for 12 minutes, or until mixture is bubbling. (The center should still be slightly jiggly; it will thicken as it cools.)

6. Remove the pan from the air fryer and sprinkle the tart with the sea salt. Cool completely on a wire rack until room temperature.

7. Transfer the pan to the refrigerator to chill. When cold (the tart will be easier to cut), use the foil overhang to remove the tart from the pan and cut into 8 wedges. Serve at room temperature.

Chocolate Chip Pecan Biscotti

Prep time: 15 minutes
Cook time: 20 to 22 minutes
Serves 10

Ingredients :

- 135 g finely ground blanched almond flour
- ¾ teaspoon baking powder
- ½ teaspoon xanthan gum
- ¼ teaspoon sea salt
- 3 tablespoons unsalted butter, at room temperature
- 35 g powdered sweetener
- 1 large egg, beaten
- 1 teaspoon pure vanilla extract
- 50 g chopped pecans
- 40 g organic chocolate chips,
- Melted organic chocolate chips and chopped pecans, for topping (optional)

Preparation Instructions :

1. In a large bowl, combine the almond flour, baking powder, xanthan gum, and salt.
2. Line a cake pan that fits inside your air fryer with baking paper.
3. In the bowl of a stand mixer, beat together the butter and powdered sweetener. Add the beaten egg and vanilla and beat for about 3 minutes.
4. Add the almond flour mixture to the butter and egg mixture; beat until just combined.
5. Stir in the pecans and chocolate chips.
6. Transfer the dough to the prepared pan and press it into the bottom.
7. Set the air fryer to 164°C and bake for 12 minutes. Remove from the air fryer and let cool for 15 minutes. Using a sharp knife, cut the cookie into thin strips, then return the strips to the cake pan with the bottom sides facing up.
8. Set the air fryer to 148°C. Bake for 8 to 10 minutes.
9. Remove from the air fryer and let cool completely on a wire rack. If desired, dip one side of each biscotti piece into melted chocolate chips, and top with chopped pecans.

Pretzels

Prep time: 10 minutes
Cook time: 10 minutes
Serves 6

Ingredients :

- 335 g shredded Mozzarella cheese
- 110 g blanched finely ground almond flour
- 2 tablespoons salted butter, melted, divided
- 50 g granular sweetener, divided
- 1 teaspoon ground cinnamon

Preparation Instructions :

1. Place Mozzarella, flour, 1 tablespoon butter, and 2 tablespoons sweetener in a large microwave-safe bowl. Microwave on high 45 seconds, then stir with a fork until a smooth dough ball forms.
2. Separate dough into six equal sections. Gently roll each section into a 12-inch rope, then fold into a pretzel shape.
3. Place pretzels into ungreased air fryer basket. Adjust the temperature to 188°C and set the timer for 8 minutes, turning pretzels halfway through cooking.
4. In a small bowl, combine remaining butter, remaining sweetener, and cinnamon. Brush ½ mixture on both sides of pretzels.
5. Place pretzels back into air fryer and cook an additional 2 minutes.
6. Transfer pretzels to a large plate. Brush on both sides with remaining butter mixture, then let cool 5 minutes before serving.

S'mores

Prep time: 5 minutes
Cook time: 30 seconds
Makes 8 s'mores

Ingredients :

- Coconut, or avocado oil, for spraying
- 8 digestive biscuits
- 2 (45 g) chocolate bars
- 4 large marshmallows

Preparation Instructions :

1. Line the air fryer basket with baking paper and spray lightly with oil.
2. Place 4 biscuits into the prepared basket.
3. Break the chocolate bars in half, and place 1/2 on top of each biscuit. Top with 1 marshmallow.
4. Air fry at 188°C for 30 seconds, or until the marshmallows are puffed, golden brown and slightly melted.
5. Top with the remaining biscuits and serve.

Blueberry Cream Cheese Bread Pudding

Prep time: 15 minutes
Cook time: 1 hour 10 minutes
Serves 6

Ingredients :

- 240 ml single cream
- 4 large eggs
- 65 g granulated sugar, plus 3 tablespoons
- 1 teaspoon pure lemon extract
- 4 to 5 croissants, cubed
- 150 g blueberries
- 110 g cream cheese, cut into small cubes

Preparation Instructions :

1. In a large bowl, combine the cream, eggs, 65 g of sugar, and the extract. Whisk until well combined. Add the cubed croissants, blueberries, and cream cheese. Toss gently until everything is thoroughly combined; set aside.
2. Place a 3-cup Bundt pan (a tube or Angel Food cake pan would work too) in the air fryer basket. Preheat the air fryer to 204°C.
3. Sprinkle the remaining 3 tablespoons sugar in the bottom of the hot pan. Cook for 10 minutes, or until the sugar caramelizes. Tip the pan to spread the caramel evenly across the bottom of the pan.
4. Remove the pan from the air fryer and pour in the bread mixture, distributing it evenly across the pan. Place the pan in the air fryer basket. Set the air fryer to 176°C and bake for 60 minutes, or until the custard is set in the middle. Let stand for 10 minutes before unmolding onto a serving plate.

Olive Oil Cake

Prep time: 10 minutes
Cook time: 30 minutes
Serves 8

Ingredients :

- 120 g blanched finely ground almond flour
- 5 large eggs, whisked
- 175 ml extra-virgin olive oil
- 75 g granulated sweetener
- 1 teaspoon vanilla extract
- 1 teaspoon baking powder

Preparation Instructions :

1. In a large bowl, mix all ingredients. Pour batter into an ungreased round nonstick baking dish.
2. Place dish into air fryer basket. Adjust the temperature to 148°C and bake for 30 minutes. The cake will be golden on top and firm in the center when done.
3. Let cake cool in dish 30 minutes before slicing and serving.

New York Cheesecake

Prep time: 1 hour
Cook time: 37 minutes
Serves 8

Ingredients :

- 170 g almond flour
- 85 g powdered sweetener
- 55 g unsalted butter, melted
- 565 g full-fat cream cheese
- 120 ml heavy cream
- 340 g granulated sweetener
- 3 eggs, at room temperature
- 1 tablespoon vanilla essence
- 1 teaspoon grated lemon zest

Preparation Instructions :

1. Coat the sides and bottom of a baking pan with a little flour.
2. In a mixing bowl, combine the almond flour and powdered sweetener. Add the melted butter and mix until your mixture looks like breadcrumbs.
3. Press the mixture into the bottom of the prepared pan to form an even layer. Bake at 164°C for 7 minutes until golden brown. Allow it to cool completely on a wire rack.
4. Meanwhile, in a mixer fitted with the paddle attachment, prepare the filling by mixing the soft cheese, heavy cream, and granulated sweetener; beat until creamy and fluffy.
5. Crack the eggs into the mixing bowl, one at a time; add the vanilla and lemon zest and continue to mix until fully combined.
6. Pour the prepared topping over the cooled crust and spread evenly.
7. Bake in the preheated air fryer at 164°C for 25 to 30 minutes; leave it in the air fryer to keep warm for another 30 minutes.
8. Cover your cheesecake with plastic wrap.

Place in your refrigerator and allow it to cool at least 6 hours or overnight. Serve well chilled.

Peach Fried Pies

Prep time: 15 minutes
Cook time: 20 minutes
Makes 8 pies

Ingredients :

- 420 g can sliced peaches in heavy syrup
- 1 teaspoon ground cinnamon
- 1 tablespoon cornflour
- 1 large egg
- Plain flour, for dusting
- Half a sheet of shortcrust pastry cut into 2

Preparation Instructions :

1. Reserving 2 tablespoons of syrup, drain the peaches well. Chop the peaches into bite-size pieces, transfer to a medium bowl, and stir in the cinnamon.
2. In a small bowl, stir together the reserved peach juice and cornflour until dissolved. Stir this slurry into the peaches.
3. In another small bowl, beat the egg.
4. Dust a cutting board or work surface with flour and spread the piecrusts on the prepared surface. Using a knife, cut each crust into 4 squares (8 squares total).
5. Place 2 tablespoons of peaches onto each dough square. Fold the dough in half and seal the edges. Using a pastry brush, spread the beaten egg on both sides of each hand pie. Using a knife, make 2 thin slits in the top of each pie.
6. Preheat the air fryer to 176°C.
7. Line the air fryer basket with baking paper. Place 4 pies on the baking paper.
8. Cook for 10 minutes. Flip the pies, brush with beaten egg, and cook for 5 minutes more. Repeat with the remaining pies.

Chocolate and Rum Cupcakes

Prep time: 5 minutes
Cook time: 15 minutes
Serves 6

Ingredients :

- 150 g granulated sweetener
- 140 g almond flour
- 1 teaspoon unsweetened baking powder
- 3 teaspoons cocoa powder
- ½ teaspoon baking soda
- ½ teaspoon ground cinnamon
- ¼ teaspoon grated nutmeg
- ⅛ teaspoon salt
- 120 ml milk
- 110 g butter, at room temperature
- 3 eggs, whisked
- 1 teaspoon pure rum extract
- 70 g blueberries
- Cooking spray

Preparation Instructions :

1. Preheat the air fryer to 176°C. Spray a 6-cup muffin tin with cooking spray.
2. In a mixing bowl, combine the sweetener, almond flour, baking powder, cocoa powder, baking soda, cinnamon, nutmeg, and salt and stir until well blended.
3. In another mixing bowl, mix together the milk, butter, egg, and rum extract until thoroughly combined. Slowly and carefully pour this mixture into the bowl of dry mixture. Stir in the blueberries.
4. Spoon the batter into the greased muffin cups, filling each about three-quarters full.
5. Bake for 15 minutes, or until the center is springy and a toothpick inserted in the middle comes out clean.
6. Remove from the basket and place on a wire rack to cool. Serve immediately.

Baked Brazilian Pineapple

Prep time: 10 minutes
Cook time: 10 minutes
Serves 4

Ingredients :

- 95 g brown sugar
- 2 teaspoons ground cinnamon
- 1 small pineapple, peeled, cored, and cut into spears
- 3 tablespoons unsalted butter, melted

Preparation Instructions :

1. In a small bowl, mix the brown sugar and cinnamon until thoroughly combined.
2. Brush the pineapple spears with the melted butter. Sprinkle the cinnamon-sugar over the spears, pressing lightly to ensure it adheres well.
3. Place the spears in the air fryer basket in a single layer. (Depending on the size of your air fryer, you may have to do this in batches.) Set the air fryer to 204°C and cook for 10 minutes for the first batch (6 to 8 minutes for the next batch, as the fryer will be preheated). Halfway through the cooking time, brush the spears with butter.
4. The pineapple spears are done when they are heated through, and the sugar is bubbling. Serve hot.

Printed in Great Britain
by Amazon

16135964R00050